A Primer of Population Biology

A Primer of
Population Biology

EDWARD O. WILSON and
WILLIAM H. BOSSERT

DEPARTMENT OF BIOLOGY, HARVARD UNIVERSITY

SINAUER ASSOCIATES, INC. PUBLISHERS
SUNDERLAND, MASSACHUSETTS 01375

17   18   19   20

Library of Congress Catalog Card Number: 73-155365

SBN: 0-87893-926-1

Published by
Sinauer Associates, Inc.
Sunderland, Mass. 01375

Contents

Acknowledgments

We are indebted to many students and colleagues whose suggestions provided the mutations and selection pressure by which the *Primer* evolved. Several fellow teachers in population biology, William L. Brown, Madhav Gadgil, Daniel H. Janzen, Bruce R. Levin, William W. Murdoch, Thomas J. M. Schopf, and David S. Woodruff reviewed part or all of this book with an eye to its practical merits. While they do not agree in full with our final selection of topics, and undoubtedly favor their own pedagogical approach to certain particular topics, their recommendations have been weighed carefully and acted on to the improvement of the final version.

How to Learn Population Biology 1

THE NECESSITY OF A QUANTITATIVE APPROACH

To the student who has not yet had much experience in mathematics and problem solving, a first glance at the *Primer* may give the impression that its subject matter is advanced and relatively difficult. This is very far from the truth. The material is elementary, and it is also fundamental to the understanding of a large part of evolutionary biology. The methods stressed are mathematical model building, measurement techniques, and problem solving, because as teachers we believe that the beginning student of biology, as well as advanced researchers, must heed Lord Kelvin's warning that "Unless you have measured it, you don't know what you are talking about." Although to apply the dictum in a blanket fashion would be unwarranted and excessive, we have noticed that much of the confusion and misunderstanding in the contemporary literature of evolutionary theory and ecology, fields that have received more than their share of polemics, arise when the disputants can't measure it. In the past, progress usually followed when ideas were abstracted into sets of parameters and relations that could be built into models or when new methods of measurement were invented. Indeed, this has been true of the history of science generally, and there is no reason to expect that any part of biology will prove to be a permanent exception. For the student who wishes to learn ideas, no valid alternative exists to mastering the derivations, from first principles, of the equations associated with the ideas. The final test of comprehension is whether he can solve numerical problems by drawing on this knowledge. Where such quantitative refinements do not exist, their invention stands as a challenge to theoretical biologists.

Nor is this book difficult. It is written so that you can learn its contents rather quickly, even without further instruction—although help from instructors should always be welcomed. For six years, Harvard students taking the elementary course in evolutionary biology were introduced to population genetics by a preprint of Chapter 2 of the *Primer*. Virtually all of them learned the material on their own, without special preparation and in the absence of lectures on the subject. They proved themselves prepared for lectures and reading on advanced topics during the second half of the course. More limited and recent trials have indicated that the same can be accomplished with the introductions to ecology and species equilibrium theory that comprise Chapters 3 and 4 of the *Primer*.

There is a second, equally compelling reason for transmitting elementary population biology in this manner. Most biology instructors encounter great difficulty in teaching mathematical techniques to biology students or even in advising them on which mathematics courses to take. We have noticed that the trouble lies not so much in the intrinsic difficulty of mathematics as in its relevance. The zealous student can work his way up into advanced calculus and statistics and still not be able to think sensibly about the simplest problems in population biology. In a symmetrical fashion, the mathematics student who wishes to enter population biology often has great difficulty visualizing problems in ways that make the problems accessible to his analytic skills. The missing piece, we believe, is that first step in creative thought—the invention of a model to describe the biological problem. To truly understand a subject you need to get a feeling of how theoreticians work. Actually, most theoretical biologists utilize only a few kinds of rather straightforward mental operations, which can be appreciated and fully comprehended by practice. Once you can deal with the subject at this level, you will lose all of your fear of it. Concepts will become enjoyable challenges capable of lucid resolutions, and mathematics might even turn out to be fun! The *Primer* is designed to try to provide this kind of experience.

Now is the time for the essential caveat which must accompany any introduction to population biology. Virtually all of the statements you are about to read are deliberate oversimplifications. Few of the formulas can be used by themselves to make exact predictions of events in nature. This will become clear very early when, passing through the section on population genetics, you learn that evolutionary events are usually controlled by multiple factors, including chance deviations of gene frequencies during reproduction. Nevertheless, this first abstract knowledge will allow you to make reasonably accurate estimates in many cases, and it will provide a good intuitive understanding of the foundations of a large part of population biology. To make this important second point clear, we will consider in a preliminary way one of the most basic ideas of ecology: the logistic curve of population growth. First, however, if you are not sure of the adequacy of your training in genetics and mathematics, you may wish to read the next section to learn more about the background required in these two subjects.

HOW MUCH GENETICS AND MATHEMATICS ARE NEEDED?

Students with a knowledge of Mendelian genetics at the level given in introductory college courses (and some high school curricula) should have no difficulty with the treatment of the subject in the section on population genetics. As for mathematics, a grasp of the elementary operations of algebra is essential. Calculus up to the level of the most elementary differential equations is useful. Most biology students should have acquired this much by the end of their first year. If you have not, you may wish to spend the several days needed to learn the requisite amount from a self-instruction text such as *Quick Calculus*, by D. Kleppner and N. F. Ramsey (John Wiley & Sons, Inc.) or its equivalent. But even in advance of that you can make some headway in the *Primer* by noting the following definitions and operations:

Δq Pronounced "delta q." Means some amount of change in the quantity of q. In this book, q is used to designate the frequency of a given gene. ΔN, to take a second example, means a change in the number of individuals (N) in the population. The Greek letter Δ, therefore, is a prefix generally used to denote a change in some variable.

$\Delta q/\Delta t$ Usually pronounced "delta q delta t." Means a certain amount of change in q during some interval of time. Thus, this term could mean a change of some amount (say, 0.3) in a year, or of this or some other amount in a generation, and so on, depending on the time scale we choose. $\Delta N/\Delta t$, to choose a second example, means a change in N with the passage of time.

$\Delta q/\Delta t = 0$ Means, of course, no change has occurred in the time interval (Δt) under consideration. A frequent step in model building is to say, "Let us see what happens at equilibrium, that is, let $\Delta q / \Delta t = 0$."

dq/dt Usually pronounced "d q d t." Means the same thing as $\Delta q / \Delta t$, except that the interval Δt, instead of being a year or a generation, is made infinitesimally small. This kind of term is the basis of all differential equations where time is the independent variable (and where we are therefore considering the change of such dependent variables as q and N through time). It means the rate at which q is changing at some instant in time—whether we are measuring the rate in amount of change per year or per generation or whatever. For example, the expression for exponential growth of a certain population might be

$$\frac{dN}{dt} = 0.03N$$

If time is measured here in years it means that at every instant the number of individuals in the population is increasing at such a rate that a 3 percent increase (that is, 0.03 of N) will be registered in a year. If time is measured in numbers of generations, it means that a 3 percent increase occurs in a generation.

$N_t = N_0 e^{0.03t}$ is the "solution" of the differential equation just given. Instead of giving just the rate of change (dN/dt), it states how many individuals (N_t) there will be in the population after a certain specified amount of time (t) has passed. N_0 is the number of individuals with which we started. The letter e signifies the constant $2.71828\ldots$, which is the base of natural logarithms. Only a course in calculus can show you how to "solve" differential equations like this one, but if at least the general relation between such equations and their solutions is clear, the reading of the *Primer* will be much easier.

It is also useful to have an elementary knowledge of statistics to use the *Primer*. What is most desired is a grasp of the following set of definitions.

MEAN   This is defined as the average or "expected" number. It can denote the simple arithmetical average. For example, the mean (the arithmetical average) of (1,2,3) is 2. That of (6,8,9,14) is 9.25. The mean can also be translated into the probability of some event occurring. Thus, if some event occurs in 0.2, or 20 percent, of all cases, we speak of the probability of its occurring in any single given case (the fate of which is not known in advance) as 0.2, or 20 percent.

VARIANCE   This is the standard measure of dispersion of the individual data around the mean. Note that the set of numbers (0,2,4) has a greater dispersion than (1,2,3), even though both have a mean of 2. The variance is the average squared difference between the individual numbers and the mean. The variance of (1,2,3) is

$$\frac{(2-1)^2 + (2-2)^2 + (2-3)^2}{3} = \frac{2}{3}$$

while the variance of (0,2,4) is

$$\frac{(2-0)^2 + (2-2)^2 + (2-4)^2}{3} = \frac{8}{3}$$

STANDARD DEVIATION   This is the square root of the variance and is symbolized by the Greek letter σ (sigma). Its great usefulness will be demonstrated as we go along.

FREQUENCY DISTRIBUTION   This is a statement of the number of individuals belonging to each class of some variable. The following is an example of a frequency distribution: Of ten men in a sample, one was less than 66 in. in height, three were from 66 to 68.9 in., four were 69 to 71.9 in., and two were over 72 in. Frequency distributions are often expressed in graphical form as shown in Figure 1. Some of them can be characterized by a general formula and thus employed analytically (as part of a series of algebraic operations). The most useful special cases in elementary population biology are the binomial distribution and Poisson distribution, which you will encounter in population genetics, and the normal distribution, which appears repeatedly in all branches of population biology. An example of the normal (bell-shaped) distribution is given in Figure 1.

If you have not done so already, you probably should plan to take a course in elementary statistics or at least to work with an elementary text such as *Statistical Methods,* by H. Arkin and R. R. Colton (College Outline Series, No. 27, Barnes and Noble, Inc., New York). Furthermore, bear in mind that the stronger the mathematical background acquired in the future,

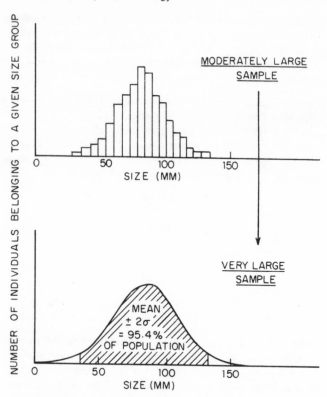

1 FREQUENCY DISTRIBUTIONS of many characteristics of a population yield bell-shaped ("normal") curves. As the number of individuals increases, the frequency curve more closely approaches the ideal form. In a "perfect" normal distribution, 68.3% of all individuals are within one standard deviation of the mean (mean $\pm \sigma$), 95.4% within two standard deviations (mean $\pm 2\sigma$), and 99.7% within three standard deviations (mean $\pm 3\sigma$).

the firmer will be your ultimate grasp of the complex and important science to which this book serves as an introduction.

HOW TO CONSTRUCT A MATHEMATICAL MODEL

In this section we will explore the subject of population growth in order to derive two of the fundamental equations associated with it. The manner of presentation is designed to illustrate the creative steps taken in the invention of the models of population biology. We believe it will help you to grasp theoretical ideas more quickly, and, of equal importance, it will disclose some of the general strengths and weaknesses of the theoretical approach.

The modeling effort must begin with a basic statement about changes in the size of a population: The rate of increase of a population is the difference between the rate of addition of individuals due to birth and immigration and the rate of subtraction due to death and emigration. We can write this statement concisely in algebraic terms by adopting shorthand symbols for all of the factors:

$$\frac{dN}{dt} = B + I - D - E$$

where N is the population size, dN/dt is the calculus shorthand for the rate of increase of N with time, and B, I, D, E are the rates at which individuals are born, immigrate, die, and emigrate.

In order to make progress beyond such an elementary proposition, it is often helpful to hold some of the factors constant, or to eliminate their influence altogether, while exploring the role of the one or two remaining. Using this method, we can make the assumption that the population is closed to the outside, so that $I = 0$ and $E = 0$ (no individuals enter the population from the outside or leave it). Such simplifying steps are common in the construction of mathematical models and have contributed markedly to the distrust many biologists have of models. Too often, it is argued, the model builder purposely ignores factors that are not insignificant to the natural system being modeled. We must recognize, however, that the omission of a particular factor at some stage in the development of a model does not imply that it is unimportant. It may instead be considered so important that an entire separate modeling effort will be applied to it later. Until it is properly considered, the modeler will merely indicate how it can be integrated into the current effort, just as we have done. The current effort, then, is comparable to a controlled experiment in which factors known to be important are eliminated from consideration by careful experimental design.

To continue with the analysis of population growth, we note that the absolute number of deaths or births in a given interval of time will depend on the number of individuals in the population. The more organisms there are, the more births or deaths there might be. As a first possibility, let us suppose that there exist some average fertilities and probabilities of death over all of the individuals in the population. This means that B and D

are each proportional to the number of individuals N. In symbols $B = bN$ and $D = dN$, where b and d are the average birth and death rates per individual per unit time. We can now write

$$\frac{dN}{dt} = bN - dN$$

or

$$\frac{dN}{dt} = (b - d)N$$

This is the equation for EXPONENTIAL POPULATION GROWTH, usually written with $(b - d) = r$. The constant r is called THE INTRINSIC RATE OF INCREASE of the population. We will not pursue the implications of the model as it now stands, except to point out that if b is greater than d, then the population size N must continue to increase without limit, and always faster and faster. Try a few numerical calculations to convince yourself of this if you have never seen the equation before. Start with some values for N and r and estimate the N after the passage of one unit of time (the same unit used for r) by the following operation, where $\times$ is the multiplication sign:

$$\text{Next } N = \text{current } N + r \times \text{current } N$$

The unit of time can be arbitrarily selected (minutes, months, years, etc.). Which unit is taken will then determine the value of r. But for our purposes you can also pick r arbitrarily. Doing this, now, convince yourself of the truth that all populations allowed indefinite exponential growth will eventually contain more organisms than there are atoms in the visible universe, and whose combined bulk will be expanding outward at the speed of light.

Of course populations do not have this capacity, so the assumptions of our model must have some serious flaw. A number of possible developments could be attempted after a reflection on why the unlimited increase seems absurd to us. There simply would not be enough food to support a population infinitely large, or space for the individuals to stand, sleep, or reproduce. How have we implicitly ignored these considerations in our model?

The problem lies in our implicit assumption that b and d were constants, with values independent of N. This is not an uncommon problem in modeling. By assigning the shorthand symbols b and d to the birth and death rates, we lost some contact with their biological meaning. One must take great care always to treat the equations as concise expressions of the

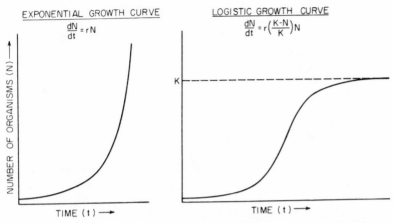

2   TWO BASIC EQUATIONS for the growth and regulation of populations (written as differential equations) and the solutions to the equations (drawn as curves).

more complex natural system and not as entities whose mathematical properties are important in their own right. Let us examine the effect of increased population size on the values of b and d. As the population increases, the death rate will probably increase due to a number of effects, such as the reduction in the average food and space available to each individual. The birth rate, on the other hand, will probably decrease with increased population size, except perhaps for small populations in which individuals are spaced so far apart they have trouble finding mates. We must express the effect of N on the birth and death rates in algebraic form if we are to add it to our model. The vague terms INCREASE and DECREASE must be made precise. Without contrary information, we will follow the modeler's usual procedure of interpreting these qualitative terms as straight-line (linear) increase and decrease. Recall that the equation for straight-line dependence of one variable, say y, on another, say x, is $y = a + bx$ where a is the intercept of the line on the y axis (for $x = 0$) and b is the slope of the line. We can therefore state the dependence of b and d on N as $b = b_0 - k_bN$ and $d = d_0 + k_dN$. In this case, b_0 and d_0 are the values approached as the population size becomes very small, k_b is the slope of the decrease for the birth rate, and k_d is the slope of the increase for the death rate. We can substitute these relationships into our model to find

$$\frac{dN}{dt} = [(b_0 - k_b N) - (d_0 + k_d N)]N$$

This is one form of the LOGISTIC EQUATION for the growth and regulation of populations. Although it looks much more complicated than its parent model, which was simply

$$\frac{dN}{dt} = (b - d)N$$

it can still be solved explicitly for N. It can also be readily employed in numerical investigations of the kind already suggested for the elementary exponential growth equation.

In addition to providing a more realistic solution for N, the form of the logistic model just derived holds a few new and interesting concepts for us. Recall that when $b = d$, the population maintains a stable size. That is, the population can maintain itself at the value of N such that

$$b_0 - k_b N = d_0 + k_d N$$

(in other words the birth rate equals the death rate), or

$$N = \frac{b_0 - d_0}{k_b + k_d}$$

This value of N is called the carrying capacity of the environment. It is usually given the shorthand symbol K. Using the equations just written, you might want to convince yourself by numerical calculations that for any value of N greater than K, the population will decrease in size. Similarly for N less than K, the population will increase. The carrying capacity K is therefore not only the upper bound of the growing population size, it is an equilibrium population size that will be approached in time from any initial population size. Finally, let us combine the two key shorthand notations that have been defined:

$$K = \frac{(b_0 - d_0)}{(k_b + k_d)}$$

and

$$r = b_0 - d_0$$

By substituting them into the form of the logistic equation just derived and rearranging the terms through several algebraic steps, we obtain

$$\frac{dN}{dt} = rN\left(\frac{K - N}{K}\right)$$

This is the familiar form, provided in most textbooks, of the logistic equation for the growth and regulation of animal populations. Usually the equation is stated flatly in this way, then the constants are defined and discussed with reference to their possible biological meaning. The derivation provided in this chapter gives the reason why population growth can be described in this particular way. We have also used the derivation to illustrate the construction of a typical mathematical model in the stepwise fashion usually employed by theoreticians. The subject of population growth will be explored in greater detail in Chapter 3.

2 Population Genetics

DEFINITION OF EVOLUTION

Evolution can be broadly defined as any change in the genetic constitution of a population. Population genetics has allowed a more precise definition: ANY CHANGE IN GENE FREQUENCY. In the simplest case, two alleles A and a occur in a population in frequencies p and q respectively. If A and a are the only alleles at the locus, then by definition $p + q = 1$. An increase or a decrease in p, therefore, means a corresponding and opposite decrease or increase in q. Suppose that we observed the following values for p and q over three successive generations: $0.60 + 0.40 = 1.0$; $0.59 + 0.41 = 1.0$; $0.57 + 0.43 = 1.0$. In this case p, the frequency of A, steadily decreased, and q, the frequency of a, steadily increased by the same amount. Now suppose that the next two successive generations underwent a reversal in the trend: $0.59 + 0.41 = 1.0$; $0.60 + 0.40 = 1.0$. This example shows that it is technically possible to have reversed evolution, at least at the level of sets of alleles. If we had taken counts only at the first and last generations, or at the second and fourth generations, the evolution would not have been observed. Most actual cases of evolution successfully analyzed have proven much more complex than this. Because most characters are under the control of multiple loci, and natural selection is also complex in nature, a complete picture can probably never be drawn from the enumeration of a few gene frequencies. Nevertheless, the systematic treatment of population genetics must start at this level.

The problems of population genetics can be reduced in their essence to two questions. FIRST, WHAT IS THE ORIGIN OF THE BASIC UNITS OF GENETIC VARIATION AT THE GENIC AND CHROMO-

SOMAL LEVELS? SECOND, WHAT ARE THE CAUSES OF CHANGES IN THE FREQUENCY WITH WHICH THESE UNITS OCCUR IN POPULATIONS? For the moment, answers to the questions can be crudely formulated as follows. New units of genetic variation originate by gene and chromosome mutations, and by new combinations of these. Mutations thus create the raw materials of evolution, but by themselves do not cause more than trivial changes in gene frequencies, unless their rates are abnormally high. The bulk of evolution at the population level, that is, changes in gene frequency, is caused by a complex of other agents, of which by far the most important is natural selection.

This capsular statement of population genetics is to a degree merely a modern rewording of the original theory of evolution by natural selection proposed in 1858 by Charles Robert Darwin and Alfred Russell Wallace. Expanded by Darwin in 1859 in his famous *The Origin of Species,* the Darwin-Wallace theory held that genetic variation arises continuously in populations by RANDOM FLUCTUATIONS in the hereditary material, while progressive evolution is impelled by natural selection of the FITTEST of the variants. This idea, commonly called Darwinism, was a major conceptual innovation. The most important earlier theory of evolution had been stated by Jean Baptiste de Lamarck in his 1809 work *Philosophie Zoologique.* Lamarck's conception of evolution was based on the false assumption that new characters acquired during the lifetime of organisms, by use or disuse of parts of the body, are passed on to the offspring:

> All that which nature has caused individuals to acquire or lose through the circumstances to which their race is exposed over a long period of time and, consequently, through the influence of predominant use or constant disuse of that part; all this is passed on to the next generation, providing the acquired changes are common to the two sexes or to those who produce the new individuals. (*Philosophie Zoologique,* vol. 1, p. 233).

Although held up to ridicule during the polemics of the early nineteenth century, the Lamarckian hypothesis of the INHERITANCE OF ACQUIRED CHARACTERS was a good one in that it offered a concrete hypothesis subject to experimental verification. But such was the spirit of the times that no fair test was made until nearly the end of the century.

In the time of Darwin and Wallace, genetics as a science had not been born. Their advanced notion of random fluctuations in the hereditary material turned out to be an adequate approximation of mutations, as these have come to be understood in the present century. The development of evolutionary biology since about 1920 is often referred to as the Modern Synthesis, or Neo-Darwinism, by which is meant that Mendelian genetics has been fused with the theory of natural selection, creating the basic discipline of population genetics. Population genetics has in turn been applied with great success to the reshaping of such related subjects as chromosome cytology, systematics, speciation theory, and biogeography. The centennial of the publication of *The Origin of Species,* celebrated in 1959 by many international conferences and by the publication of memorial compendia, saw the Modern Synthesis still in full progress.

CHARACTERISTICS OF MUTATIONS

A MUTATION is defined as a heritable change in the genetic material, and a MUTANT is the changed organism that results. A distinction is made between POINT MUTATIONS and CHROMOSOME ABERRATIONS. The former involve changes too minute to be observed by any existing form of microscopy. Genetic and biochemical analyses using bacteria have confirmed that point mutations are molecular events involving substitutions of one nucleotide pair for another in the DNA molecule. At the other end of the scale, the chromosome aberrations involve major structural changes that can be observed under the light microscope. Such alterations encompass not one but hundreds or thousands of nucleotide pairs. Probably the easiest way to envisage the various kinds of chromosome aberrations is to visualize a stick of putty as a rough structural model of the chromosome. The aberrations are the analogs of virtually everything that can be done to the putty stick short of twisting it out of shape. It can be broken up to create a larger number of smaller sticks (INCREASE IN CHROMOSOME NUMBER). It can be joined to another putty stick (FUSION leading to REDUCTION IN CHROMOSOME NUMBER). One can take a piece out of the stick (DELETION); insert an extra piece (DUPLICATION); remove a piece, flip it over, and reinsert it (INVERSION); transfer a piece to another stick (TRANSLOCATION); or exchange non-homologous pieces with another stick (RECIPROCAL TRANSLOCATION). In company with other sticks representing a complete diploid $(2n)$ set of chromosomes, the following additional changes can be simulated. A single stick can be added to the set, giving a total of $2n + 1$ (the cell is then called a TRISOMIC) or taken away, giving a total of $2n - 1$ (the cell is then called a MONOSOMIC). The conditions of trisomy and monosomy are referred to generically as ANEUPLOIDY. It is also possible to replicate the entire set of sticks one or many times over, giving an exact multiple of the haploid number; this condition is called POLYPLOIDY. The polyploid series is labeled in sequence, after haploid for n and diploid for $2n$, as follows: $3n$ (triploid), $4n$ (tetraploid), $5n$ (pentaploid), $6n$ (hexaploid), $7n$ (septaploid), $8n$ (octoploid), and so on; in practice, Greek adjectives are seldom applied to higher multiples than 8. Most of the major classes of chromosome aberrations are illustrated in Figure 1. All play some role in evolution. Inversion and polyploidy are especially significant in the magnitude of their effects and frequency with which they occur in nature. The distinction between chromosome aberrations and point mutations is that the aberrations are simply structural changes that can be seen, so that the lower limit of the magnitude of the change observed is set by limitations in microscopy and not by innate structural properties of the chromosomes. Furthermore, our present understanding of the molecular structure of DNA leads us to infer that (1) the alterations at the nucleotide level causing point mutations are of the same structural nature as chromosome aberrations and (2) the segments of DNA involved may vary in length from a single nucleotide pair continuously up to dimensions great enough to be observed by microscopy, at which level they become easily classifiable as chromosome aberrations.

Three general properties of point mutations and chromosome aberrations of prime significance in population genetics will now be considered.

Chemical process. Mutations can ultimately be described as alterations in the sequence of nucleotide pairs in the DNA polymer. While it is possible that some such alterations may occur during periods when the DNA is not being replicated, many lines of evidence suggest that most spontaneous mutations are copy errors that occur in the course of DNA replication. In particular, mutation is fastest when cell divisions are taking place, and a rise in temperature increases the rate of the two processes to about the same degree. Mutations act like molecular events in several important ways. First, mutation rates increase very regularly with temperature. In fact the Q_{10}, or rate of increase of the mutation rate over a $10°C$ increase in temperature, usually lies between 2 and 3; this relation is exemplified in Figure 2. Mutations can be induced by high energy radiation, such as x-rays. The number of induced mutants is a simple linear function of the dosage, also as illustrated in

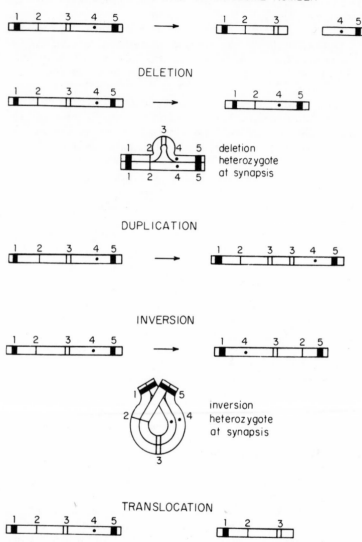

INCREASE IN HAPLOID CHROMOSOME NUMBER

DELETION

deletion
heterozygote
at synapsis

DUPLICATION

INVERSION

inversion
heterozygote
at synapsis

TRANSLOCATION

1   MAJOR CLASSES of chromosome aberrations. When these altered chromosomes synapse with normal homologs at the onset of the first meiotic division, they assume characteristic configurations that permit locus-by-locus matching. Two of the synaptic configurations, those of the deletion and of the inversion, are also illustrated.

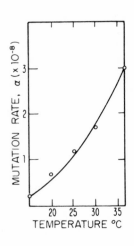
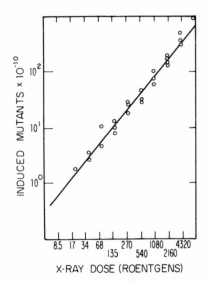

2   MUTATION RATE in the bacterium *E. coli* increases with temperature and ionizing radiation. Curve at left shows the effect of temperature on the incidence of mutation *his−* (inability to synthesize histidine) to *his+* (ability to synthesize it). Curve at right shows the number of *met-2+* mutants (able to synthesize methionine) induced by exposing *met-2−* colonies (nonsynthesizers) to increasingly large doses of x-rays. (*Based on Sager and Ryan, 1961*).

Figure 2. For every measured amount of dose the same number of mutations are induced according to the equation

$$M = kD$$

where M is the number of mutants, D is the dose of the radiation, and k is a dose-independent constant describing the sensitivity of the unmutated gene. This simple relation between x-ray dosage and mutation rate has given rise to the so-called target theory, which pictures the gene as a target which, when subjected to a sufficient number of x-ray–induced ionizations, mutates in a single step. The theory is consistent with the notion that point mutations are unitary molecular events.

Mutations can also be induced by chemical MUTAGENS. The mutagens are easiest to demonstrate in experiments on microorganisms. For the student with some background in biochemistry, the following technical details will help clarify the nature of the process. Certain alkylating agents that mimic radiation in their effects, such as the sulfur and nitrogen mustards, probably generate mutations by causing breaks in the polynucleotide strands. Others, such as certain purines, caffeine, and adenine, and unnatural analogs of pyrimidines, induce copy errors at the level of the nucleotide pair. Nitrous acid acts as a mutagen in a more straightforward manner. By oxidative deamination, it substitutes an hydroxyl for an amino group and thereby converts the DNA and RNA bases into new forms, for example,

Cytosine   Uracil

Randomness. Randomness is uncertainty. A random event is one whose occurrence cannot be predicted with certainty. We can at best hope to predict the *probability* of its occurrence. In real life, we can successfully treat many processes as though they were random even though they could equally well be regarded as deterministic if we knew more about them. Coin flipping is a good example. Under normal circumstances we cannot predict the outcome of any single flip. But we do know that approximately half of all coins turn up heads and half tails. Similarly, any single unbiased coin flipped many times in succession gives the same result. We are thus able to make certain predictions about the outcomes of experiments with coins. By using the binomial distribution based on the binary event (head versus tail), it is possible to predict the probabilities of occurrence of various ratios of heads and tails in an infinitely varying number of trials. For example, the probability of getting exactly 31 heads and 19 tails in 50 trials is given by the formula for the binomial distribution as

$$\frac{50!}{31!19!} (0.5)^{50} = 0.027$$

However, note that in spite of our use of the idea of randomness, it really would be possible to predict the outcome of any given coin flip if only we knew enough in advance about the specific details of the mechanics of the finger motion, the air density and currents, and the structure of the surface on which the coin lands. As long as these factors are variable and unknown, it is reasonable to consider the outcome of the total coin flipping experiment as a random event. The two treatments represent separate levels of explanation.

The same considerations hold for the occurrence of mutations. If in a "thought experiment," we had the improbable power of measuring in an instant of time the physical and chemical state of a mutable gene and its microenvironment, we could presumably then specify whether a mutation was about to occur. At the molecular level, such knowledge is possibly denied us by the uncertainty principle of physics, which states that at the atomic level to observe directly is to alter the outcome significantly. But even if it were not, our studies of population phenomena compel us to inquire whether we can describe sets of mutations as random events, for the chief interest of evolutionary studies is in mass (population) processes rather than in molecular events.

The following experiment exemplifies in a simple and elegant manner the general technique by which the randomness of mutations can be tested. It was performed by F. J. Ryan (Sager and Ryan, 1961). When bacteria (*Escherichia coli*) that cannot use lactose are grown on an amino acid medium, mutants appear (at the rate of 2×10^{-7} per cell division) that can use the sugar. On the surface of agar containing amino acids combined with lactose, the nonutilizing parents form a colony. The mutants arising within the colony, also by using the lactose present, overgrow to form papillae on the colony surface. When a certain indicator dye is incorporated in the medium, the lactose-utilizing papillae turn red because they form specific waste products that react with the dye. Meanwhile, the colony background remains almost white, allowing a ready enumeration of the papillae. Because of its discrete location and conformity of shape, each papilla is judged to contain the offspring of a single mutant. The question is: Does each of the nonutilizing colonies have an equal chance of producing a lactose-utilizing mutant? Since the microenvironments of each of the colonies is assumed to be the same, this is the equivalent of asking whether the mutation occurs at random with respect to colonies. The data obtained in the experiment were immediately susceptible to a standard statistical test. Since the mutation is a very rare event but the number of bacteria per colony is very great, the frequency distribution of mutations per colony should approximate a Poisson distribution. That is,

$$p(x) = \frac{m^x}{x!} e^{-m}$$

where $p(x)$ is the probability that x papillae (i.e., mutants) will occur per colony, m is the mean number of papillae per colony, and e is the natural constant 2.71828. . . . Ryan's data are shown in Figure 3. The mean number of papillae per colony was 0.57. The Poisson distribution can now be calculated with $m = 0.57$ and $x = 0, 1, 2, 3$ respectively. As shown in the same figure, the "fit" of the expected Poisson curve and observed curve is very close, giving support to the hypothesis that the lactose-utilizing mutations do indeed occur at random with respect to colonies.

Preadaptation. The property of randomness in mutations has a major consequence in evolutionary theory. It leads to the conclusion that mutations occur without reference to their future adaptiveness in the environment. In other words, within a population with a certain genetic constitution, a mutant is no more likely to appear in an environment in which it would be favored than one in which it would be selected against. When a favored mutation appears, we can therefore speak of it as exhibiting true PREADAPTATION to that particular environment. That is, it did not arise as an adaptive response to the environment but rather proves fortuitously to be adaptive after it arises. Natural selection, i.e., differential survival and reproduction in the environment, then becomes the primary determinant of the frequency of the mutant gene in subsequent generations.

Abundant experimental evidence exists to document the preadaptive nature of some mutants. One especially effective test was made in experiments on *E. coli* by J. and E. M. Lederberg. These geneticists were interested in learning whether mutants resistant to bacteriophage and streptomycin occur in cultures not exposed to these bactericidal agents. First, they cultured nonresistant strains on agar free of the agents, then lowered a sterile piece of velvet onto the agar plate so that the fine hairs of the fabric picked up cells from each of the colonies present. The fabric with its adhering cells now could be used in REPLICA PLATING in a fashion analogous to making impressions from an inked rubber stamp. That is, when lowered onto a new agar plate, the fabric transferred cells to the same positions as on the original plate. When the new plate contained streptomycin or bacteriophage, new colonies formed only at loci where, on the original plate, colonies of resistant bacteria had existed. That such mutants really had existed on the original plate was

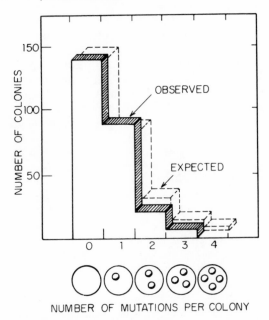

NUMBER OF MUTATIONS PER COLONY

3 FREQUENCY DISTRIBUTION of lactose-utilizing mutations in colonies of *E. coli* (*shaded*) compared with the Poisson distribution (*broken line*) having the same mean. The probability of drawing a sample in which the mutations were distributed according to a Poisson distribution is 0.2. This value is high enough to support (but not to prove) the hypothesis that the two distributions are the same. (*Modified from Sager and Ryan, 1961*).

proven by fixing their position on the plate by comparison with the replica plate, removing cells from these original colonies, and finally successfully culturing them in other media containing bacteriophage or streptomycin.

A second technique used to prove the preadaptation hypothesis in both microorganisms and higher organisms (flies of the genus *Drosophila*) is INDIRECT SELECTION. This test can be applied both to new mutations and to pre-existing genetic variation. Organisms from the same parent are divided into two groups of sibs, one of which is exposed to some toxic agent and one of which is not. Only unexposed individuals are used to start the next generation. In particular, the unexposed individuals chosen are the ones that are derived from the same parents as the exposed individuals which displayed respectively the best and the poorest resistance to the poison. Thus, the generations are perpetuated by lines subjected to selection but not to actual exposure to the toxin. If mutants (or gene forms already present) were not preadaptive but rather required direct exposure in order to appear and increase, then indirect selection would have no effect on the resistance of the untested stocks. This turns out not to be the case. The untested stocks are as much modified genetically as the stocks subjected to direct selection. It is therefore necessary to revert to the hypothesis of preadaptation.

Low rates. In Table I are given mutation rates from a diversity of organisms. One generalization can safely be made from these data: The great majority of mutations occur at the rate of 10^{-5} per gene per replication or less. It is also necessary to conclude that the sample exhibited must be greatly biased to favor detection of those mutations which occur most frequently. Mutation rates much lower than 10^{-9} (and there must be a great many in this class) cannot be expected to be measured at all, even in the fast-multiplying microorganisms. Moreover, it is unsafe to assume that the cause of a given phenotypic change is always exactly the same, that is, that a given new phenotype is always due to exactly the same mutant allele wherever the phenotype makes its appearance in the population. In many cases, closer analysis reveals the existence of series of ISO-ALLELES (alleles that produce very similar phenotypes), where only one allele was thought to exist before. The phenotypic products, in fact, may seem to differ solely through slight differences in the properties of certain enzymes or other proteins which can be ordinarily detected only by electrophoretic separation. Where enzymes are involved, such minor variants are sometimes called ISOZYMES. The detection of protein varieties by electrophoresis has proven an invaluable means of directly measuring some kinds of genetic variation in natural populations. Inspection of Table I shows that most known mutations in microorganisms occur from 10^{-6} to 10^{-9} per cell per replication, whereas they are several orders of magnitude higher in multicellular organisms. Rates in the two groups are not exactly comparable, since in multicellular organisms mutants in germinal lines accumulate through time, and the older the organism the more numerous the mutant cells. However, even in mammalian tissue cultures, where rates can be calculated per cell generation, the rates are still relatively high.

It is a reasonable assumption that mutation rates are under genetic control subject to modification by natural selection. MUTATOR GENES exist (e.g., in *Drosophila*) that alter the mutation rates at other loci, and they may be responsible for

I. A SAMPLE OF SPONTANEOUS MUTATION RATES
IN DIFFERENT ORGANISMS
(From Sager and Ryan, 1961)

Organism / Character	Rate	Units
BACTERIOPHAGE — T2		
Lysis inhibition, $r \rightarrow r^+$	1×10^{-8}	Per gene* per
Host range, $h^+ \rightarrow h$	3×10^{-9}	replication
BACTERIA — *Escherichia coli*		
Lactose fermentation, $lac^- \rightarrow lac^+$	2×10^{-7}	
Histidine requirement, $his^- \rightarrow his^+$	4×10^{-8}	
$his^+ \rightarrow his^-$	2×10^{-6}	Per cell per
Streptomycin sensitivity,		division
$str\text{-}s \rightarrow str\text{-}d$	1×10^{-9}	
$str\text{-}d \rightarrow str\text{-}s$	1×10^{-8}	
ALGAE — *Chlamydomonas reinhardi*		
Streptomycin sensitivity,		
$str\text{-}s \rightarrow str\text{-}r$	1×10^{-6}	
FUNGI — *Neurospora crassa*		Mutant fre-
Inositol requirement, $inos^- \rightarrow inos^+$	8×10^{-8}	quency among
Adenine requirement, $ade^- \rightarrow ade^+$	4×10^{-8}	asexual spores
CORN — *Zea mays*		
Shrunken seeds, $Sh \rightarrow sh$	1×10^{-5}	
Purple, $P \rightarrow p$	1×10^{-6}	
FRUIT FLY —		
Drosophila melanogaster		
Yellow body, $Y \rightarrow y$, in males	1×10^{-4}	Mutant fre-
$Y \rightarrow y$, in females	1×10^{-5}	quency per gam-
White eye, $W \rightarrow w$	4×10^{-5}	ete per sexual
Brown eye, $Bw \rightarrow bw$	3×10^{-5}	generation
MOUSE — *Mus musculus*		
Piebald coat color, $S \rightarrow s$	3×10^{-5}	
Dilute coat color, $D \rightarrow d$	3×10^{-5}	
MAN — *Homo sapiens*		
Normal → hemophilic	3×10^{-5}	
Normal → albino	3×10^{-5}	
HUMAN BONE — Marrow cells		
in tissue culture		
Normal → 8-azoguanine resistant	7×10^{-4}	Per cell per
Normal → 8-azoguanosine resistant	1×10^{-6}	division

* Correction of the other mutation rates in this table to per-gene basis would not change their order of magnitude.

occasional extraordinary rates as high as 10^{-2} per cell per generation.

Reversibility. If mutations are normal chemical processes, we should expect them to be reversible at some regular rate. This is the case. By convention, FORWARD MUTATIONS are those from the "normal" or wild type to the mutant condition; RE-VERSE or BACK MUTATIONS restore the mutant to the wild type. In *Drosophila melanogaster*, for example, a gene for eye color mutates from the normal bright red condition (W) to a paler condition (W^e) and back again at the rates shown below.

$$W \underset{4.2 \times 10^{-5}}{\overset{1.3 \times 10^{-4}}{\rightleftarrows}} W^e$$

THE MAGNITUDE OF MUTATIONS

Depending on the degree of the resulting phenotypic altera-tion, a distinction is sometimes made among various degrees of evolution, e.g., microevolution, mesoevolution, and macroevo-lution. The magnitude of the change is roughly correlated with the number of chromosomal loci involved and the number of successive allelic changes taken in each. Simple cases of micro-evolution might involve no more than substitution of one allele for another in a population, whereas such an extreme case of macroevolution as the descent of birds from Mesozoic reptiles almost certainly entailed many successive substitutions at loci on all of the chromosomes. Of course the extreme possi-bility has been entertained, as in Richard Goldschmidt's famous "hopeful monster" theory of the 1930s, that large-scale evolu-tion can take place in one genetic step by means of a single overwhelming macromutation. Extraordinary new phenotypes are occasionally produced by spontaneous mutations. Examples include the *homeotic mutants* of insects, in which appendages are transformed into new kinds of appendages: antennae into legs (the aristapedia mutant), wings into legs, halteres into wings, and so forth. But there is no evidence that such extreme forms ever survive to give rise to new taxa. On the contrary, the empirical evidence shows that the greater the effects of a mu-tation the more likely it is to be poorly adapted or even lethal. The reason for this inverse correlation can be illuminated by use of the "clock analogy." Most populations in nature, like most timepieces in good working order, are at any moment operating not perfectly but at least near the optimum permitted by the limitations of their basic construction. A mutation is a random alteration in the genetic regulation of this operation. It can be likened to a randomized change in the machinery of the clock such as an arbitrary tightening, loosening, or even removal of a spring. The result might be to bring the regulation closer to the permissible optimum, but the odds are strongly in favor of the opposite happening. And the greater the alteration, the more likely the mechanisms will move away from the optimum. Theoretically it may be possible to create a bird from a reptile in one scrambling alteration of the chromosomes. But this is but one of a near infinitude of possible results of such a random major mutation, almost all of which would be quite lethal, and the chance of its occurring is therefore close to zero. We are led to infer that most major evolutionary changes occur by the gradual accumulation of minor mutations, accompanied by very gradual phenotypic transitions; and so far as it is known the fossil record seems to confirm this notion.

STABILITY OF GENE FREQUENCIES

No ordinary cellular event is more complex and far-reaching in its consequences than gametogenesis. In diploid organisms, the crucial step is the first meiotic division, during which the homologous chromosomes come together in synapsis, exchange segments, and then separate into different daughter cells. We may well ask what effect gametogenesis, together with the subsequent restoration of the diploid condition in syngamy, have on the frequencies of the genes. In short, does the scrambling of the genes through segregation and recombination cause evolution? The answer is that it does not. The gene frequencies remain stable, and the frequencies of the diploid genotypes can be readily predicted from them.

To understand why this is so, first examine the idealized life cycle of a diploid organism shown in Figure 4. Since the basic Mendelian laws of heredity are followed, the set of interbreeding individuals is referred to as a MENDELIAN POPULATION. We can add for convenience the condition of PANMIXIA. A panmictic population is one in which mating is random with respect to the specific genes in question—each physiologically competent individual has an equal chance of mating with any physiologically competent member of the opposite sex. Consider the relative frequencies, p of allele A, and q of allele a, where $p + q = 1$. We wish to know whether events in the life cycle will alter p and q, and what will be the frequencies of the diploid genotypes AA, Aa, and aa.

Since the population is panmictic, the gametes are mixed at random. Each gamete carries either A or a. In order to predict

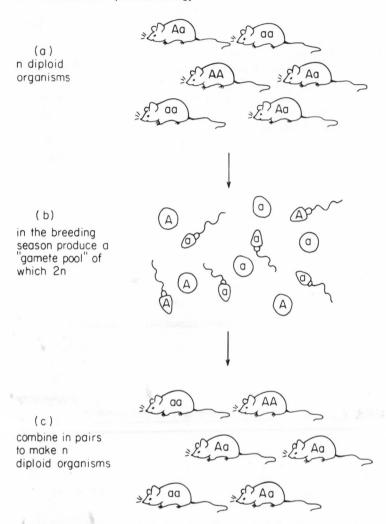

(a)
n diploid
organisms

(b)
in the breeding
season produce a
"gamete pool" of
which 2n

(c)
combine in pairs
to make n
diploid organisms

4   IDEALIZED LIFE CYCLE of a diploid organism. Here *n* diploid organisms (*top*) in the breeding season produce a "gamete pool" (*center*). 2*n* gametes combine in pairs to make *n* diploid organisms (*bottom*). Segregation and recombination cause no net change in gene frequencies and, hence, do not cause evolution.

the diploid frequencies based on p of A and q of a, we take advantage of a basic theorem of probability theory: THE PROBABILITY OF THE UNION OF INDEPENDENT EVENTS IS EQUAL TO THE PRODUCT OF THEIR SEPARATE PROBABILITIES. In other words,

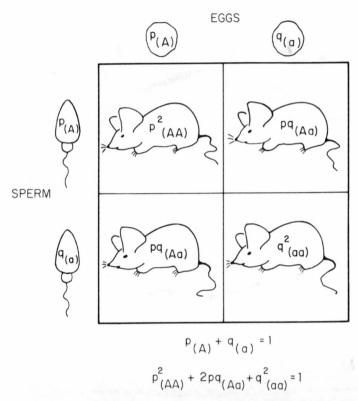

$$p_{(A)} + q_{(a)} = 1$$

$$p^2_{(AA)} + 2pq_{(Aa)} + q^2_{(aa)} = 1$$

5   BASIS OF HARDY-WEINBERG EQUILIBRIUM. The multiplication matrix shows the frequencies of all of the possible combinations.

if p is the probability (= frequency) of the A-bearing gametes, which is also the frequency of the A genes in the whole pan-mictic population, the probability of bringing two A gametes together at fertilization is simply $p \times p = p^2$. The multiplication matrix of Figure 5 displays the frequencies of all of the possible combinations. Here the identities of the diploid geno-types (AA, Aa, aa) are given as subscripts to their respective proportions. Summing up the entries in the matrix, and recalling that the total equals unity, we obtain

$$p^2_{AA} + 2pq_{Aa} + q^2_{aa} = 1$$

The same result can be obtained as follows:

$$(p_A + q_a)^2 = p^2_{AA} + 2pq_{Aa} + q^2_{aa} = 1$$

since $p + q = 1$, and unity squared is unity. This is the equation for a binomial distribution for sets of two. In genetics it is called the HARDY-WEINBERG FORMULA, or Hardy-Weinberg "law," after the mathematician (G. H. Hardy) and the biologist (W. Weinberg) who first independently applied it to biology in 1908. It follows that if more than two alleles are involved, whose frequencies are $p, q, r, s, \ldots$, the diploid frequencies can be estimated from the multinomial distribution:

$$(p + q + r + s + \ldots)^2 = 1$$

In most mathematical models, the frequencies $(q + r + s + \ldots) = 1 - p$ are treated in sum as a single frequency (labeled as q) to simplify the distribution to the binomial case. In practice the method suffices to treat frequencies of single alleles as opposed to all these others in the same locus.

From the binomial distribution it is easy to show that the gene frequencies remain constant from generation to generation. From $p^2 + 2pq + q^2 = 1$, we take the fraction contributed by p:

$$\text{Frequency of } A \text{ in next generation} = \frac{p^2 + pq}{p^2 + 2pq + q^2} = p^2 + pq = p^2 + p(1 - p) = p$$

By symmetry it follows that the frequency of a in the next generation will be q. Thus the original gene frequencies are preserved.

A characteristic of panmictic Mendelian systems is that no matter what the starting frequencies of the diploid genotypes, they will conform to the binomial distribution in the next generation and each generation thereafter. For example, suppose that we began by mixing 6,000 AA individuals with 4,000 aa individuals. The starting diploid frequencies would be aa 0.60, Aa 0, aa 0.40; also, $p = 0.6$ and $q = 0.4$. In the next generation and every generation thereafter, the distribution can be expected, if we ignore deviations due to pure sampling error, to fit the binomial distribution. The frequency of AA would be $p^2 = 0.36$; the frequency of Aa, $2pq = 0.48$; and the frequency of aa, $q^2 = 0.16$. The frequency of the A allele will be $0.36 + \frac{1}{2}(0.48) = 0.36 + 0.24 = 0.60$, the starting frequency.

PROBLEM. Vestigial wings in *Drosophila* are controlled by a single recessive gene. In a certain population 10^{-4} of the adults are found to have vestigial wings. Predict the frequency of heterozygotes that will exist in the early stages of the next generation (that is, before further natural selection occurs).

ANSWER. If the frequency of the homozygous recessives is labeled q^2 in accordance with convention, then q, the predicted frequency of the recessive allele in the next generation, is the square root of 10^{-4}, or $(10^{-4})^{1/2} = 0.01$. The predicted frequency p of the dominant allele is therefore $1 - 0.01 = 0.99$, and the predicted frequency of the heterozygotes is $2pq = 0.0198$.

PROBLEM. The organic compound phenylthiocarbamide (PTC) tastes very bitter to most persons. The inability to taste PTC is controlled by a single recessive gene. In the American white population, about 70 percent can taste PTC and 30 percent cannot. Estimate the frequencies of the taster (T) and nontaster (t) genes in this population, as well as the frequencies of the diploid genotypes.

ANSWER. The datum of use is q^2, the frequency of tt persons, which is 0.30. The square root of 0.30 is $q = 0.55$, which is the estimated frequency of the t allele. The frequency of the T allele can then be estimated as $p = 1 - q = 0.45$, the frequency of the homozygote tasters (TT) as $p^2 = 0.20$, and the frequency of the heterozygote tasters (Tt) as $2pq = 0.50$.

The Hardy-Weinberg equilibrium is the starting theorem in the theory of evolutionary genetics. In the study of real populations, it is used to test hypotheses of panmixia and evolutionary stasis. If a population is both panmictic and undergoing no evolutionary change the diploid frequencies will fit (within reasonable limits of sampling error) the binomial distribution based on the observed gene frequencies. If its frequencies deviate significantly, it is necessary to examine for evidence of (1) nonrandom mating among the genotypes, such as a preference of individuals for mates of their own genotype or (2) a change in the frequencies due to one of the evolutionary agents to be described in subsequent sections, or both. If, on the other hand, the distribution is reasonably close to the binomial, this fact by itself does not prove panmixia and stasis. Unusual patterns of evolutionary change can occur that also yield the binomial distribution. Finally, various degrees of inbreeding or genetic change can occur which are significant in evolutionary time but too small to detect in the samples chosen.

THE SIGNIFICANCE OF SEXUAL REPRODUCTION

The genetic effect of normal sexual reproduction is to create new diversity in the diploid stage at each generation. It is immensely effective in this role. In the case of asexual organisms, in which no recombination occurs, the only way for a population to increase its variability is through new mutations or immigration of new types from the outside. When normal sexual reproduction is added, new combinations of genes can be assembled on the same chromosome through crossing over during each act of gametogenesis. Since the organisms are in addition diploid for at least the early part of their existence, even more new combinations of chromosomes can be assembled at each fertilization. The collaboration of crossover, which generates new combinations of genes on the same chromosome, and independent assortment, which changes combinations of chromosomes, produces a virtually endless genetic diversity. In the simplest case of an allele system, two alleles on one locus produce just three diploid genotypes: *AA, Aa, aa.* If we add a second locus with two alleles, nine genotypes are possible: *AABB, AABb, AAbb, AaBB, AaBb, Aabb, aaBB, aaBb, aabb.* The possible number of diploid genotypes containing n such loci is 3^n. Generally, the number of genotypes is the product $m_1 m_2 m_3 \cdots m_n$ of the m_i diploid genotypes that can be constructed at each of the n loci. In most Mendelian populations, the number of loci is very large. For instance, in both *Drosophila melanogaster* and man, it has been estimated that on the order of 10,000 or more loci exist, many bearing numerous alleles. The total number of conceivable diploid genotypes in such a genome is astronomical; in fact, in the two species just named it is greater than the number of all the atoms in the visible universe! Thus, in a kaleidoscopic fashion, the sexual species exposes a new array of genotypes to the environment at each generation, while keeping its basic elements, the alleles, and their respective frequencies about the same. As a result, populations of sexually reproducing organisms enjoy an adaptability in the face of a changing environment far beyond the reach of the asexual species. This seems to be the reason why sexuality is universal, and why it has been relinquished only in a few groups of organisms with peculiar requirements, such as the need to reproduce very rapidly, that can set asexual reproduction at a premium.

THE AGENTS OF EVOLUTION

Sexual reproduction, with its attendant powers of recombination, does not impel changes in gene frequencies. Five other agents can be shown to cause this effect:

1. Mutation pressure
2. Meiotic drive
3. Gene flow
4. Selection
5. Genetic drift

The first four are deterministic, that is, they involve directions and rates that can be measured in populations and used to predict specific outcomes. In the classical mathematical theory of population genetics, developed mostly by R. A. Fisher, J. B. S. Haldane, and S. Wright in the 1920s, these forces were treated as operating on infinitely large populations of organisms, much as mathematical physics treats populations of particles as if they were infinite. The results are good for first approximations only. Populations of organisms are obviously finite, and often they are quite small. The corrective factor in the elementary theory has been the concept of genetic drift, also introduced in the 1920s. Drift encompasses all of the changes due to sampling error in finite populations. Its role in conjunction with the deterministic forces has been mathematically one of the most challenging aspects of evolutionary theory to date. In the sections to follow, each of the evolutionary agents will be considered in turn.

For purposes of orientation, let us reconsider at this point the relation between theory and observation. The mathematical theory is based on the elementary Mendelian laws of genetics, which are taken as postulates. Each of the agents is treated in models in terms of parameters, e.g., mutation rate and selection coefficient, which are related by equations and can be varied arbitrarily to disclose their relative importance in altering gene frequencies under a wide variety of conceivable conditions. The models are valuable in determining lower and upper limits of functions, i.e., the least and greatest changes that can be due to the agents under any condition. They can also be used to predict outcomes of specific real situations, such as rates of changes at various frequencies and the attainment or nonattainment of equilibria, and in this way the theory itself can be tested and improved. The purpose of mathematical theory, then, is to deal with "all possible worlds." The purpose of experimental and field population genetics is to deal with the real world: To measure the parameters, to search for new parameters, and to improve the theory which is ultimately our most effective way of viewing the real world.

The question is often raised, why not stay with the real world and generalize our experiences in some succinctly descriptive form? The only answer is that such an approach never proves adequate. In evolutionary biology, it produces inductive generalizations that are encapsulated as tendencies or "rules." Thus, northern races of mammals and birds tend to be larger than southern races of the same species (Bergmann's rule), and gross evolution tends to be irreversible (Dollo's law). Causal explanations, the heart of any science, are hard to reach and often impossible to prove by means of such concepts. The descriptive, natural history stage of science is eventually replaced by a deductive theoretical stage, basically mathematical in nature, which creates the abstractions and measurements necessary to deepen causal analysis.

For a sharper comparison of the two approaches, consider how they might be applied to an explanation of gravitation. The natural history explanation would note that there is a strong tendency for free objects to fall to the ground, at varying velocities to be specified and that birds, airplanes, and celestial bodies form exceptions. Deductive theory would concern itself with models of mass and acceleration that can be applied to all objects, both falling and in flight. The purely descriptive approach accounts for many situations but could lead us to the facile conclusion that gravitation is not universal. The theoretical approach, therefore, is needed to establish the universality and predictiveness of gravitation as the key to celestial mechanics.

One further preliminary generalization about population genetics as a science can be made which will be useful in your orientation. Because of their inherent practical difficulties, experimental studies currently lag far behind mathematical theory. Field studies, sometimes referred to as ECOLOGICAL GENETICS, are even farther behind; indeed, this important branch of population biology is still very much in its infancy. Most of the controversies in recent years over evolutionary theory do not concern pure theory at all but rather the magnitude in real populations of the parameters defined in the theory. For example, the numerous polemics in recent literature concerning the importance of genetic drift really originates from our ignorance concerning the magnitude of natural selection and gene flow in real populations. Once the selection coefficient, input from gene flow, and population size in a given system are specified, there is little room for disagreement concerning the effect of sampling error. Only more empirical information than is now available from laboratory and field studies will allow us to generalize about populations as a whole. You should try to distinguish clearly in your own mind the relation between general theory and empirical evidence relating to specific cases while approaching each of the topics to follow.

MUTATION PRESSURE

As mutations occur, they not only provide new genetic material on which the other evolutionary agents can act, but by necessity they also alter gene frequencies to some extent. Whether that extent is ever more than trivial is arguable. It is at least conceivable that mutations can sometimes occur so frequently and so strongly in one direction as to force substitution of one gene after another. Imagine the existence of a series of alleles in which high, unidirectional mutation rates are linked one to the other:

$$a_1 \rightarrow a_2 \rightarrow a_3 \rightarrow a_4$$

If unopposed by other significant evolutionary forces, all populations would eventually stabilize as homogeneously a_4. Such an extreme phenomenon if realized would be a mechanism of ORTHOGENESIS, or predetermined straight-line evolution unaffected by influences in the environment. The original concept of orthogenesis was applied to larger evolutionary changes observed in fossil lineages. It was based on inadequate evidence that gave the false impression of unidirectionality. Vitalistic and entirely nongenetic in origin, this primitive concept of orthogenesis has now been almost wholly abandoned. Genetic orthogenesis as conceived in our model is feasible but extremely unlikely. To see clearly why this is so, we need to construct the model in a more analytical fashion. Let p be the frequency of some allele a_1 mutating at the rate of some fraction μ per generation to a second allele a_2. The rate of change of the frequency as just stated can be expressed as

$$\frac{dp}{dt} = -\mu p \qquad [1]$$

where t is measured in number of generations. In other words, the rate at which the gene frequency is changing is simply a fraction of the frequency at the instant of time we measure the change. The constant μ is called the MUTATION RATE. The solution of the differential equation is the elementary exponential decay equation, obtained as follows:

$$\frac{dp}{p} = -\mu dt$$

$$\int \frac{dp}{p} = -\int \mu dt$$

$$\ln p = -\mu t + \ln c$$

$$p = ce^{-\mu t}$$

Setting $p = p_0$ as the starting frequency of a_1 when $t = 0$, we obtain $c = p_0$, and

$$p = p_0 e^{-\mu t} \qquad [2]$$

Note that since a_1 is mutating to a_2 its frequency p is decreasing whereas q, the frequency of a_2, is gaining. Since $p + q = 1$,

$$q = 1 - p_0 e^{-\mu t}$$

Recall from Table I that μ for most mutations is 10^{-4}/cell/generation or less. By substituting this number into Equation 2, we see that the number of generations must equal the reciprocal of μ in order to reduce p to a fraction e^{-1}, or approximately one-third, of p_0 (since $e = 2.71828 \ldots$). In other words, most mutations would require on the order of 10,000 generations to reduce the gene frequency to one-third of its original value, and more than twice this amount of time to reduce it to one-tenth. Moreover, Equation 2 may give too large a rate of change. It requires that neither reverse mutation to a_1 nor any other evolutionary agent be operating to a significant degree. Such circumstances are highly unlikely in multicellular organisms, where a single gene substitution at the maximum rate would consume hundreds or thousands of years. In microorganisms with generation times covering only minutes or hours, on the other hand, such a change might require only days. As yet our knowledge of microbial population dynamics is still too incomplete to permit a judgment as to whether significant evolution can really occur in this way under natural conditions.

It is useful at this point to introduce the notion of GENETIC EQUILIBRIUM by use of the mutation pressure model. In this case the MUTATIONAL EQUILIBRIUM is sought. Let μ and v (the Greek letters mu and nu) represent forward and reverse mutation rates between a_1 and a_2.

$$a_1 \underset{v}{\overset{\mu}{\rightleftharpoons}} a_2$$

This time let us follow changes in q, the frequency of a_2. Its change per generation, Δq, is the gain in forward mutations from a_1 to a_2 (μp), minus the loss in reverse mutations from a_2 to a_1 (vq), or

$$\Delta q = \mu p - \nu q = \mu(1 - q) - \nu q \qquad [3]$$

At the *equilibrium frequency* $\hat{q}$ (pronounced "q hat"), $\Delta q = 0$ by definition, that is, at equilibrium there is no change. Setting $\Delta q = 0$ and solving for $\hat{q}$ in Equation 3, we get

$$\hat{q} = \frac{\mu}{\mu + \nu}$$

The symmetrical result is obtained for $\hat{p}$. Dividing one equation by another we obtain

$$\frac{\hat{q}}{\hat{p}} = \frac{\mu}{\nu}$$

PROBLEM. In *Salmonella* bacteria, there exist antigenic phases, which are strains differing from each other by single genes and with such similar phenotypes that they can be identified only by the most sensitive techniques, such as antigen-antibody reactions in rabbits' blood. In very large populations of the kind that exist in pure laboratory cultures, mutations from one phase to the other can be readily measured. In one case analyzed by B. A. D. Stocker, mutations occurred from one phase (let us call it a_1) to a second phase (a_2) at the rate of 5.2×10^{-3}, while the reverse mutation occurred at the rate of 8.8×10^{-4}. Predict the equilibrium frequencies of the two phases.

ANSWER. The system can be better visualized by utilizing the following diagram:

$$a_1 \underset{\nu\,=\,8.8\,\times\,10^{-4}}{\overset{\mu\,=\,5.2\,\times\,10^{-3}}{\rightleftharpoons}} a_2$$

Let q be the frequency of a_2 and p be the frequency of a_1. Then

$$\hat{q} = \frac{\mu}{\mu + \nu} = 0.86$$

$$\hat{p} = 1 - \hat{q} = 0.14$$

These are within 1 percent of the values actually obtained in laboratory experiments.

MEIOTIC DRIVE

If one allele is included in more than one-half of the successful gametes from heterozygotes, the allele can increase in frequency even if it has a harmful effect. Unequal gamete production, when attributable purely to the mechanics of meiosis, has been called MEIOTIC DRIVE. The effect is difficult in practice to distinguish from GAMETIC SELECTION, which is the differential mortality of cells during the period between the reductional division of meiosis and zygote formation. Gametic selection is best regarded under the rubric of natural selection. True meiotic drive has been studied as an evolutionary force only in the past 15 years; a formal treatment is given by Crow and Kimura (1970). The distribution and general significance of the phenomenon is not yet known.

The most extensively studied example is the segregation distorter locus (SD) of Drosophila melanogaster. The locus is located in the centromeric heterochromatin of chromosome II. Males heterozygous for the SD locus transmit it in great excess, whereas heterozygous females exhibit normal segregation. The meiotic drive in this case appears to stem from some interaction between the SD and SD+ (normal) chromosomes during synapsis. When synapsis in the male is prevented by the proximity of other chromosome abnormalities, the segregation is normal. It is also probably significant that males do not display chromosome crossover. Although the SD chromosome occurs in some natural populations, it is uncommon (under 10 percent), leading to the conclusion that it is subject to some as yet unspecified adverse selection pressure. The low frequencies are probably in dynamic equilibrium determined by selection acting on the offspring of meiotic drive. In such a circumstance, one expects that any additional genes able to combat the *SD* effect by reducing the distorting power of the locus would be favored by selection. In fact, it has been discovered that there is a greater prevalence of *SD*-insensitivity among *SD*+ alleles in populations where the *SD* locus exists than where it is absent.

GENE FLOW

Together with natural selection, the swiftest way by which gene frequencies can conceivably be altered is by introducing into the population groups of genetically different individuals. Let a population (which we will label α), containing a frequency q_α of a certain allele, receive some fraction m of its individuals in the next generation from a second population (called β) with a frequency q_β of the same allele. To speed your intuitive grasp of the process, examine the diagram in Figure 6 depicting the effect of immigration on the frequency (q_α) of the white allele in an imaginary population of butterflies.

Population α, with a frequency of q_α of the white allele,   receives a fraction m of its population   each generation from population β, with a frequency q_β of the white allele.

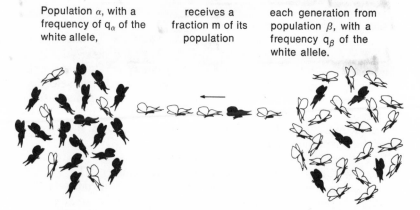

6   EVOLUTION BY GENE FLOW. Population α (*left*), with a frequency of q_α of white alleles, receives a fraction (*m*) of its individuals from population β (*right*), which has a frequency q_β of white alleles.

By inspection it can be seen that the frequency of the allele in population α is then altered to the frequency of the allele in the nonimmigrant part of the population (q_α) times the proportion of individuals that are not immigrants ($1 - m$), plus the frequency of the same allele among the immigrants (q_β)

times the proportion of individuals in the population that are new immigrants (m). The altered frequency (q'_α) is thus

$$q'_\alpha = (1 - m)q_\alpha + mq_\beta$$

and the amount of change in one generation is

$$\Delta q = q'_\alpha - q_\alpha = -m(q_\alpha - q_\beta) \qquad [4]$$

Please derive this equation on your own to increase your understanding of it. Then if you will insert a few imaginary figures and note the resulting Δq, it will become clear to you that only a small difference in gene frequencies (of the magnitude that often separates populations), together with a moderate migration coefficient (m), is needed to effect a significant evolutionary change. The phenomenon is referred to as GENE FLOW or MIGRATION PRESSURE. Two categories can be distinguished: INTRASPECIFIC GENE FLOW between geographically separate populations of the same species; and INTERSPECIFIC HYBRIDIZATION. The former occurs constantly within many plant and animal species and is a major determinant of the patterns of geographic variation. Interspecific hybridization occurs during breakdowns of normal species-isolating barriers. Ordinarily it is temporary, or at least rapidly shifting in nature. Although much less common than gene flow within species, it has a greater effect because of the larger number of gene differences that normally separate species.

NATURAL SELECTION: GENERAL PRINCIPLES

Natural selection is simply THE DIFFERENTIAL CHANGE IN RELATIVE FREQUENCY OF GENOTYPES DUE TO DIFFERENCES IN THE ABILITY OF THEIR PHENOTYPES TO OBTAIN REPRESENTATION IN THE NEXT GENERATION. The variation in competence can stem from many causes: Different abilities in direct competition with other genotypes; differential survival under the onslaught of parasites, predators, and changes in the physical environment; variable reproductive competence; variable ability to penetrate new habitats; and so on. Any of these selective phenomena, when effective to some degree, singly or in combination with others, constitutes natural selection. Differential reproduction means only that one genotype is increasing at a greater rate than another; stated more exactly, dn/dt varies among genotypes. The absolute growth rate is meaningless in this regard; all of the tested genotypes may be increasing or decreasing in absolute terms while nonetheless differing in the degree of increase or decrease. Natural selection is so broadly defined as to be a synonym for genetic adaptation in populations. Acting upon genetic novelties created by mutation, it is the agent that directs the course of most evolution by means of the adaptation of populations.

A selective force may act on the variation of a population in several radically different ways. The principal ensuing patterns are illustrated in Figure 7. In the diagrams, the phenotypic variation, measured along the horizontal axis, is given as normally distributed, with the frequencies measured along the vertical axis. Normal distributions are common but not universal among continuously varying characters. STABILIZING SELECTION (sometimes called OPTIMIZING SELECTION) can involve a disproportionate elimination of extremes, with a consequent reduction of variance; the distribution "pulls in its skirts" as shown in the left-hand pair. This pattern of selection occurs in all populations. Variance is enlarged each generation by mutation pressure and possibly also by immigrant gene flow; stabilizing selection constantly reduces the variance about the optimal "norm" best adapted to the local environment. Balanced polymorphism is effected by a special, very simple kind of stabilizing selection. As illustrated in a simple two-allele system, the heterozygote Aa is favored over the homozygotes AA and aa, and each generation sees a reduction in the number of homozygotes. But the gene frequencies remain constant, and as a result the same diploid frequencies recur in each following generation, in a Hardy-Weinberg equilibrium, prior to the action of selection. True DISRUPTIVE SELECTION (sometimes called DIVERSIFYING SELECTION) is a rarer phenomenon, or at least one less well known. It results from the existence of two or more accessible adaptive norms along the phenotypic scale, perhaps combined with preferential mating between individuals of the same genotype. Recent experimental evidence suggests that it might occasionally result in the creation of new species. DIRECTIONAL SELECTION (or DYNAMIC SELECTION, as it is sometimes called) is the principal pattern through which progressive evolution is achieved. It will be dealt with in detail in the next section.

One should bear in mind that selection always acts on phenotypes. For evolution to occur it is necessary for phenotypic distributions of the kind schematized in Figure 7 to be determined at least in part by genetic variation. If it were not, each new generation, being genetically uniform with respect to the phenotype, would spring back to the original distribution that existed before selection operated. A great deal of applied population genetics, particularly in plant and animal breeding, is

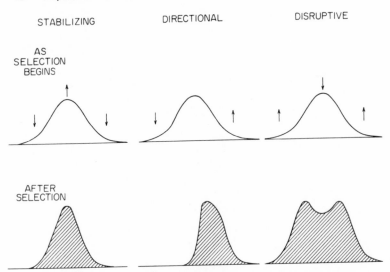

7   RESULTS OF ADVERSE (↓) AND FAVORABLE (↑) SELECTION pressures on various parts of the population frequency distribution of a phenotypic character. The ordinates (vertical axes) represent the frequencies of individuals in the populations, and the abscissas (horizontal axes) the phenotypic variation. The top figure shows the pattern as the selection begins; the bottom figure shows the pattern after selection.

devoted to this aspect of selection. The proportion of the total variance in the phenotype of a given character that is attributable to the average effects of genes in a particular set of environmental circumstances is called the HERITABILITY of the character. It is symbolized as h^2 (which stands for the heritability itself and not its square) and is defined as the ratio of the additive genetic variance (V_G) to phenotypic variance (V_P):

$$h^2 = \frac{V_G}{V_P}$$

The speed with which evolution occurs when a given amount of selection is applied is a direct function of the heritability. We will return to this concept later when the evolution of traits controlled by multiple genes is considered.

When selection takes place in a typical Mendelian population its immediate genetic consequence is to alter the frequencies of the diploid genotypes. This in turn alters the gene frequencies. Selection does not act directly on genes, however, and the measures of selection intensity apply to diploid fre-

II. ESTIMATING FITNESS FROM DATA TAKEN BEFORE AND AFTER SELECTION WITHIN THE SAME GENERATION

NUMBER OF INDIVIDUALS IN EACH GENOTYPE
(Obtained by counting)

	AA	Aa	aa
Before selection	4,000	5,100	2,300
After selection in the same generation	3,800	4,200	1,200

SURVIVAL RATE

λ_{AA} survival rate of $AA = 3,800/4,000 = 0.95$

λ_{Aa} survival rate of $Aa = 4,200/5,100 = 0.82$

λ_{aa} survival rate of $aa\ = 1,200/2,300 = 0.52$

RELATIVE FITNESS
(Compared with AA, the most fit)

W_{AA} fitness of $AA = \lambda_{AA}/\lambda_{AA} = 0.95/0.95 = 1.00$

W_{Aa} fitness of $Aa = \lambda_{Aa}/\lambda_{AA} = 0.82/0.95 = 0.86$

W_{aa} fitness of $aa = \lambda_{aa}/\lambda_{AA} = 0.52/0.95 = 0.55$

SELECTION COEFFICIENT

s_{AA} selection coefficient of $AA = 1 - W_{AA} = 0$

s_{Aa} selection coefficient of $Aa = 1 - W_{Aa} = 0.14$

s_{aa} selection coefficient of $aa = 1 - W_{aa} = 0.45$

quencies rather than to gene frequencies. The effects on gene frequencies can readily be deduced from these measures by appropriate methods.

The measures of selection in a Mendelian population can be understood by a study of the hypothetical numerical example given in Table II. One starts with counts of individuals classified according to the DIPLOID genotypes under consideration. The arbitrary numbers used here might be estimates of the entire population. Proportions based on random sampling from the population serve just as well. By sampling immediately before and immediately after the event of selection an estimate of λ, the SURVIVAL RATE, is obtained for each genotype. For example, if the selective agent is some parasite or change in the physical environment that is effective on larval stages, the genotypic frequencies in the egg and adult stages of the same generation may be used. The ratios of the rates give the RELATIVE FITNESSES of the respective genotypes. In the traditional theory of population genetics, the fitness (W) of a genotype is defined with reference to the fitness of another by computing the ratios in this way. It is most convenient to take the genotype with the largest λ (in our case λ_{AA}) as the standard of comparison. The largest λ is used as the denominator, with the result that fitness always ranges from 0 to 1. If a smaller λ is used in the denominator, as it sometimes is in practice, fitness could vary from 0 to $+ \infty$. The result will obviously be cumbersome in some instances. Fitness has the clear intuitive meaning of relative rate of survival. The SELECTION COEFFICIENT (s) is defined as $1 - W$ and has the intuitively satisfying meaning of relative decrease due to selection.

Now turn to Table III. If recombination of genes, through sexual reproduction, occurs between organisms (for example, if the genotypic frequencies are evaluated in the mating populations of successive generations) the survival rate of one genotype can influence the frequency of more than one genotype. In this case relative fitness can be estimated by comparing observed frequencies in the second sample to those expected on the basis of the Hardy-Weinberg formula discussed previously. The ratio of these two values for any genotype is the corrected rate of proportion increase, R, for the genotype. This rate can be used in place of the survival rate in the calculation of fitness. Table III illustrates the procedure in detail.

It is quite necessary to understand the exact definitions of fitness and the selection coefficient before going on in evolutionary theory. We suggest that you study the calculations in Tables II and III, then take the initial data (under "Number of individuals in each genotype") and derive the selection coefficients yourself to make sure you grasp the entire procedure.

DIRECTIONAL SELECTION: QUANTITATIVE THEORY

To treat the quantitative aspect of directional selection, it is instructive to start with the extreme case of the systematic complete elimination of the recessive homozygotes. Employing the same notation as before for the two-allele system A and a, we may now define the fitness of aa as 0 and its selection coefficient as $1 - 0 = 1$. For simplicity let us assume that AA and Aa have the same fitness, then by definition each has a fitness of 1 and a selection coefficient of 0. This is a useful case with which to begin the study of selection because it is the only

III. ESTIMATING FITNESS FROM DATA TAKEN IN THE FIRST GENERATION BEFORE SELECTION, AND IN THE SECOND GENERATION AFTER SELECTION HAS OCCURRED

NUMBER OF INDIVIDUALS IN EACH GENOTYPE
(Obtained by counting)

	AA	Aa	aa	Total
Mating population of first generation (before selection)	3,000	3,900	2,000	8,900
Mating population of second generation (after selection)	3,800	4,400	1,800	10,000

GENE FREQUENCY IN FIRST GENERATION
(For calculating expected frequency in second generation in the absence of selection)

$$p \text{ frequency of } A = \frac{6,000 + 3,900}{17,800} = 0.56$$

$$q \text{ frequency of } a = 1 - p = 0.44$$

CORRECTED RATE OF INCREASE
(Ratio of actual number in the second generation to the number expected in the absence of selection)

$$R_{AA} \text{ rate of increase of } AA = \frac{3,800}{p^2 \times 10,000} = \frac{3,800}{0.31 \times 10,000} = 1.23$$

$$R_{Aa} \text{ rate of increase of } Aa = \frac{4,400}{2pq \times 10,000} = \frac{4,400}{0.50 \times 10,000} = 0.88$$

$$R_{aa} \text{ rate of increase of } aa = \frac{1,800}{q^2 \times 10,000} = \frac{1,800}{0.19 \times 10,000} = 0.95$$

RELATIVE FITNESS
(Compared with AA, the most fit)

$$W_{AA} \text{ fitness of } AA = R_{AA}/R_{AA} = 1.23/1.23 = 1.00$$

$$W_{Aa} \text{ fitness of } Aa = R_{Aa}/R_{AA} = 0.88/1.23 = 0.72$$

$$W_{aa} \text{ fitness of } aa = R_{aa}/R_{AA} = 0.95/1.23 = 0.77$$

SELECTION COEFFICIENT

$$s_{AA} \text{ selection coefficient of } AA = 1 - W_{AA} = 0$$

$$s_{Aa} \text{ selection coefficient of } Aa = 1 - W_{Aa} = 0.28$$

$$s_{aa} \text{ selection coefficient of } aa = 1 - W_{aa} = 0.23$$

IV. COMPLETE ELIMINATION OF RECESSIVES

	AA	Aa	aa	Frequency of a
Before selection	p_0^2	$2p_0q_0$	q_0^2	$q_0 = q_0$
After selection	$\dfrac{p_0^2}{p_0^2 + 2p_0q_0}$	$\dfrac{2p_0q_0}{p_0^2 + 2p_0q_0}$	0	$q_1 = \dfrac{q_0}{1+q_0}$

one in which the gene frequency q_n can be derived after n generations of selections as a simple algebraic function of q_0, the starting frequency. The equation is derived in the following way. The proportions of the diploid genotypes before and after selection in a large panmictic population are given in Table IV. Following the elimination of the q^2 homozygous recessives in the model, the heterozygotes comprise $2p_0q_0$ of the surviving fraction, which is $p_0^2 + 2p_0q_0$. All of the a genes in the next generation will be contributed by these heterozygotes. Half of the gametes produced by the heterozygotes will carry a; the new fraction of a alleles, now written q_1 with the subscript indicating passage of one generation, is therefore calculated as follows:

$$q_1 = \frac{p_0q_0}{p_0^2 + 2p_0q_0} = \frac{q_0}{1+q_0} \qquad [5]$$

The relationship of q_n from one generation to the next is recursive. In other words, by using the same procedure as above for subsequent generations we obtain

$$q_2 = \frac{q_1}{1+q_1} \qquad q_3 = \frac{q_2}{1+q_2} \qquad q_4 = \frac{q_3}{1+q_3}$$

and in general, one sees that

$$q_n = \frac{q_{n-1}}{1+q_{n-1}} \qquad [5a]$$

Substituting Equation 5 into the recursive series, one term at a time as we go to generation 2, then to generation 3, and so on, we obtain

$$q_n = \frac{q_0}{1+nq_0} \qquad [6]$$

Equation 6 is often cited to prove that eugenics would be a slow and inefficient process if directed at the homozygotes alone. Suppose that mankind really decided to rid itself of an undesirable gene by passing a law preventing homozygous carriers from having children. The gene frequency would drop at a disappointingly slow rate. After many millennia, it would still persist at low frequencies. More precisely, by rearranging Equation 6 we can express the number of generations required to achieve a given change in frequency as follows:

$$n = \frac{q_0 - q_n}{q_0 q_n}$$

$$= \frac{1}{q_n} - \frac{1}{q_0}$$

PROBLEM. The initial frequency of a completely recessive gene in a population is 0.5. What is the maximum change in frequency that can be achieved in ten generations if selection is the only evolutionary agent involved?

ANSWER. The maximum change will occur if all of the homozygote recessives are removed each generation, or at least none succeed in reproducing. In that case the frequency of the gene after ten generations will be

$$q_{10} = \frac{q_0}{1 + 10 q_0} = \frac{0.5}{1 + 10 \times 0.5} = 0.083$$

and the amount of change that will have occurred is

$$q_{10} - q_0 = 0.083 - 0.5 = -0.417$$

In other words, the frequency of the gene will have dropped from 50 percent to 8.3 percent, a decrease of 41.7 percent.

PROBLEM. Albinism in human beings is controlled by a single recessive gene. Suppose that a racially homogeneous nation contained one albino among every 10,000 persons (not an unusually high figure among real populations), and it wished to reduce the frequency of the gene because of the ill effects of the trait on the health of the homozygous carriers. If all albinos voluntarily agreed to avoid having children, how many generations would it take for the occurrence of albinism to be reduced to one in a million persons?

ANSWER. The present frequency of the albino phenotype is 10^{-4} and the target frequency is 10^{-6}. These numbers are q_0^2 and q_n^2 respectively, so that the present allele frequency (q_0) is 10^{-2} and the target allele frequency (q_n) is 10^{-3}. The number of generations required to go from q_0 to q_n is $n = 1/q_n - 1/q_0 = 1,000 - 100 = 900$ generations.

PROBLEM. In the space below, draw a curve showing the

decline in the frequency of the albino gene through time for, say, a couple of thousand generations. Measure q_n along the vertical axis and n along the horizontal. Four or five points should suffice to show the shape of the curve.

Next let us consider cases where the directional selection is less drastic. In other words, s is less than 1, and W ($= 1 - s$) is greater than zero. The proportions of genotypes in a large panmictic population before and after selection are given in Table V. To make the notation less cumbersome the subscript ($_0$) is omitted from p and q, the gene frequencies in the starting generation. In the next generation the frequency of the recessive gene becomes

$$q_1 = \frac{pq + q^2(1 - s)}{1 - sq^2} = \frac{q(1 - sq)}{1 - sq^2} \qquad [7]$$

Merely by changing subscripts it can be seen at once that the relation is recursive, and that in general

$$q_n = \frac{q_{n-1}(1 - sq_{n-1})}{1 - sq_{n-1}^2} \qquad [8]$$

No solution exists to the sequence, except in the case where $s = 1$, yielding Equation 6. We are limited to expressing Δq, the increment in q in one generation:

V. PARTIAL SELECTION AGAINST RECESSIVES

	AA	Aa	aa	Total
Proportion before selection	p^2	$2pq$	q^2	1
Fitness (W)	1	1	$1-s$	
Proportion after selection	p^2	$2pq$	$q^2(1-s)$	$1-sq^2$

$$\Delta q = q_1 - q = \frac{-sq^2(1-q)}{1-sq^2} \qquad [9]$$

For small values of s, $1 - sq^2$ can be replaced by 1 without introducing much error (of more than a factor of sq^2), and the relation is approximately

$$\Delta q \doteq -sq^2(1-q)$$

This can be rewritten as a differential equation by replacing Δq with dq/dt:

$$\frac{dq}{dt} \doteq -sq^2(1-q) \qquad [10]$$

This says that q is decreasing at a rate approximately equal to its selection coefficient multiplied by the term $q^2(1-q)$. One immediate consequence, already indicated in the consideration of the special case of complete removal of recessive homozygotes, is that as q approaches 0 or 1, Δq becomes very small. The complete expression of Equation 10 is given in Figure 8.

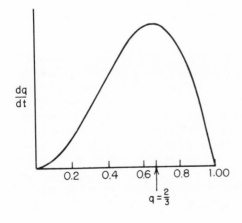

8 GRAPHICAL REPRESENTATION of the equation $dq/dt \doteq -sq^2 (1 - q)$, where the value of q is varied along the horizontal axis and where s, the selection coefficient, is held constant. (*From Li, 1955*).

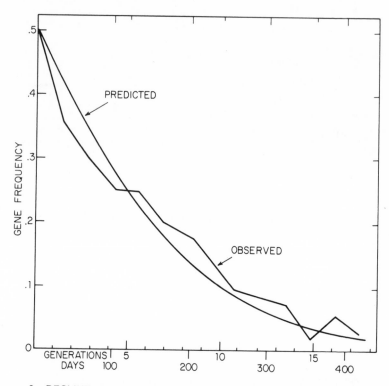

9   DECLINE IN FREQUENCY of the "raspberry" eye color gene in
a laboratory population of *D. melanogaster*. (*From Falconer, 1960,
based on data from D. J. Merrell, 1953*).

One can quickly check that dq/dt is at a maximum when q is
⅔, by taking the derivative of Equation 10, setting it equal to
zero, and solving for q. This result is important to note, for it
means, among other things, that when a favorable gene appears
in the population, it spreads very slowly at the beginning. An
actual case of change in gene frequency due to constant negative selection is shown in Figure 9. In a laboratory experiment,
D. J. Merrell allowed the recessive sex-linked gene "raspberry"
in *Drosophila melanogaster* to compete with the normal gene
over a period of about eighteen generations. Counts were made
at about monthly intervals. Meanwhile, direct study showed that
mutant and wild-type phenotypes have about the same viability,
but mutant males are only 50 percent as successful in mating.
The changes in gene frequency were predicted on the basis of

this fitness value, taking into account the added complication of sex linkage. The close fit between the predicted and observed curves was obtained when an average generation length of 24 days was assumed. Thus, the data were consistent with the theory of selection expressed in the mathematical equations.

The number of generations required to change the frequency by a certain amount may be determined from Equation 10. In particular, we may wish to predict the number of generations (n) required to alter q_0 to q_n, given a fixed selection coefficient s. Rewriting Equation 10 as

$$\frac{dq}{q^2(1 - q)} = -s \, dt$$

$$\int_{q_0}^{q_n} \frac{dq}{q^2(1 - q)} = -s \int_0^n dt = -sn$$

The left-hand integral conforms to a common form whose solution is given in standard mathematical tables:

$$sn = \left[\frac{1}{q} + \ln \frac{(1 - q)}{q} \right]_{q_0}^{q_n} \qquad [11]$$

where $\ln$ = natural logarithm. The notation on the right-hand side means that one solves the term within the brackets by inserting the value of q_n, obtaining a first number; then the bracketed term is solved by inserting the value of q_0, yielding a second number. When the second number is subtracted from the first, the value of the entire expression is obtained.

PROBLEM. Calculate the rate of change of the frequency of a from the survivorship data of Table VI. Also predict the number of generations required to reduce the frequency to 0.10, assuming the selection pressure to hold constant. Finally, predict the rate of change when $q = 0.10$.

	VI.		
	AA	Aa	aa
Before selection	500	400	100
After selection (same generation)	490	392	60

ANSWER. Following the procedure outlined in Table III, we find $s_{AA} = s_{Aa} = 0$; $s_{aa} = 0.388 \doteq 0.4$. The exact change in frequency over the interval covered by the data given, assuming that the whole population was represented, is

$\Delta q = (q$ after selection$)$ minus $(q$ before selection$)$

$$\Delta q = \frac{\frac{1}{2}(392) + 60}{942} - \frac{\frac{1}{2}(400) + 100}{1{,}000} = -0.0282/\text{generation.}$$

The theoretical change for a very large population with $q = 0.3$ and $s_{aa} = 0.4$ is, from Equation 10,

$$dq/dt \doteq -sq^2(1 - q) \doteq -(0.4)(0.3)^2(0.7) \doteq$$
$$-0.0252/\text{generation,}$$

which is close enough to the true figure to justify rounding off s_{aa} to 0.4 and employing the simplified version of the differential equation. From Equation 11 we next calculate the number of generations required to reduce the frequency from 0.3 to 0.1 as

$$sn = 0.4n = \left[\frac{1}{q} + \ln \frac{1-q}{q} \right]_{0.3}^{0.1}$$

$$n = 20$$

At $q = 0.1$ the rate of change can be predicted (again from Equation 10) as

$$\Delta q \doteq -sq^2(1 - q) \doteq -(0.4)(0.1)^2(0.9) \doteq -0.0036/\text{generation}.$$

In addition to the two cases of complete dominance just investigated, there exists a vast range of possibilities in which dominance is incomplete and the heterozygote is subjected to an intermediate degree of selection. Symbolically, if the fitness of the unfavored homozygote is $1 - s$, where $s > 0$, then the fitness of the heterozygote is $1 - ks$, where $0 < k < 1$. The simplest case would be for the heterozygote to have exactly intermediate fitness, with $k = \frac{1}{2}$ and $W_{Aa} = 1 - \frac{1}{2} s$. To derive the rate of change equation we merely proceed as before, substituting the new fitness values in Table VII. The new frequency is obtained and q subtracted from it:

$$\Delta q = \frac{pq(1 - \frac{1}{2}s) + q^2(1 - s)}{1 - sq} - q = \frac{-\frac{1}{2}sq(1 - q)}{1 - sq} \qquad [12]$$

The treatment of modifications of these basic formulas, in two-factor and other special cases, is given in Li's (1955) book and other texts in mathematical population genetics.

VII. INTERMEDIATE DEGREE OF SELECTION
AGAINST HETEROZYGOTES ($k = \frac{1}{2}$)

	AA	Aa	aa	Total
Proportion before selection	p^2	$2pq$	q^2	1
Fitness	1	$1 - \frac{1}{2}s$	$1 - s$	
Proportion after selection	p^2	$2pq(1 - \frac{1}{2}s)$	$q^2(1 - s)$	$1 - sq$

At this point you will have gained an effective insight into basic procedure followed in constructing models in classical population genetics. Let us now move on to a consideration of the interaction of the evolutionary factors.

JOINT EFFECTS OF MUTATION AND SELECTION

Once the equations are given which define the relation of the individual parameters μ, m, and s to changes in gene frequencies, equations can easily be written that express the joint action of evolutionary forces. Take for example the interaction of mutation pressure and selection. In a large, completely isolated population, we would expect these two to be the only important evolutionary forces. The change in the frequency, Δq, of an allele a can be predicted as the sum of changes due to mutation and selection separately. The frequency of q increases at the rate of $\mu(1 - q)$ per generation, where μ is the rate of mutation from other alleles to a. In the case of complete dominance q decreases by selection at the approximate rate of $-sq^2(1 - q)$ per generation. Combining these terms,

$$\Delta q = \mu(1 - q) - sq^2(1 - q) \qquad [13]$$

If mutation and selection are antagonistic, q will approach an equilibrium value $\hat{q}$, where $\Delta q = 0$. Therefore setting Δq in Equation 13 equal to zero we obtain

$$s\hat{q}^2(1 - \hat{q}) = \mu(1 - \hat{q})$$

$$s\hat{q}^2 = \mu$$

$$\hat{q}^2 = \mu/s$$

$$\hat{q} = \sqrt{\frac{\mu}{s}} \qquad [14]$$

It is intuitively satisfying, but by no means obvious without the aid of the model, to find that the mutation rate (which applies to genes) and the selection coefficient (which applies to a genotype, in this case the homozygous recessive) have equal influence in determining the equilibrial frequency. Since most mutation rates are on the order of 10^{-4} per generation, or less, it is clear that mutation pressure can hold sway only if the selection pressure is very weak—far weaker than has been found to be true in the majority of cases of microevolution analyzed to date.

JOINT EFFECTS OF GENE FLOW AND SELECTION

PROBLEM. Write the formula for the amount of change in the frequency of a recessive allele due to the interaction of gene flow and selection. Assume that other evolutionary factors have a negligible effect. Evaluate your formula with respect to its possible biological meaning.

ANSWER. We already showed (Equation 4) that gene flow into the population increases (or decreases) the frequency of the allele at the rate of $-m(q_\alpha - q_\beta)$, where m is the proportion of individuals in the recipient population that are immigrants, q_α is the frequency of the allele before immigration, and q_β is the frequency of the allele in the donor population. We also proved earlier (Equation 10) that the frequency of the allele is decreasing at the approximate rate of $-sq_\alpha^2(1 - q_\alpha)$ each generation, where s is the selection coefficient of the homozygote. The amount of change per generation is simply the sum of these two terms

$$\Delta q_\alpha = -m(q_\alpha - q_\beta) - sq_\alpha^2(1 - q_\alpha)$$

There are several ways to evaluate the biological meaning of this formula. One of the easiest and most meaningful steps is to recall that evolution through selection of homozygous recessives is most rapid when $q = \frac{2}{3}$. At this point $\Delta q = 0.15\ s$. (Both of these statements are easily verifiable directly from the selection term just given.) It follows that if the difference between the donor population and the population that receives immigrants is 0.15 or greater, gene migration is at least equally potent in evolution, and usually more so, than selection pressures of equal magnitude. This theoretical inference supports the opinion, held by most evolutionists, that gene flow generally ranks with selection as one of the two most important directing forces in evolution.

PROBLEM. At a single genetic locus there are two alleles A and a. Suppose that in a small isolated area the allele a is recessive lethal. In the rest of the world, however, the two alleles are maintained at equal frequencies $p = q = 0.5$. What fraction of the isolated area's total population must be exchanged with the outside world in each generation to maintain the allele a at an equilibrium frequency of 0.1 in the isolated population?

ANSWER. Since q is at equilibrium,

$$\Delta q_\alpha = -m(q_\alpha - q_\beta) - sq_\alpha^2(1 - q_\alpha) = 0$$

We know that $\hat{q}_\alpha = 0.1$, $\hat{q}_\beta = 0.5$, and $s = 1$; and this is all the information we need to estimate m, the fraction of individuals in the recipient population that are of immigrant origin. Inserting the known values in the equilibrium formula, we obtain $m = 0.0225$. Notice that this relatively low immigration rate sustains a much higher equilibrium frequency. This will always be the case, provided the allele is recessive—and therefore partly protected from the selection process each generation.

BALANCED POLYMORPHISM

Up to this point we have considered systems of two competing alleles in the same locus. In a constant environment one allele eliminates the other, or else the frequencies of the two are carried to some intermediate equilibrium point between zero and one by the countervailing forces of selection, gene flow, and mutation pressure (with meiotic drive a remotely possible fourth factor). However, even in the absence of a balance between the primary evolutionary agents, two or more alleles can be maintained together in the same panmictic population for indefinite periods of time. This condition is referred to as balanced polymorphism. There are several means by which such a balance can be achieved. For example, it can occur through FREQUENCY-DEPENDENT SELECTION: The fitnesses of the two alleles are not constant, but change with their frequency. If one allele has a lower fitness than the other while it is at higher frequencies, but gains the advantage when its frequency descends to a certain level, the frequency will tend to stabilize at about that level. A second condition, generally considered to be the prevailing one in natural populations, is HETEROZYGOTE SUPERIORITY. (The same condition is sometimes referred to loosely in the literature as "overdominance" or "heterotic effects" at the gene level.) It is easy to see that if a heterozygote Aa is superior to both homozygotes AA and aa, neither allele can eliminate the other. We can further expect the frequency of a (written as q) and the frequency of A (p, which is by definition $1 - q$) to stabilize at some intermediate frequency between 0 and 1.

Table VIII provides the minimal set of values required for constructing a model of evolution due to heterozygote superiority. We are interested in computing the equilibrial value $\hat{q}$, that is, the value of q at which the selection process against the two homozygotes come into balance, and $\Delta q = 0$. The calculation of the formula for the equilibrium value from the model proposed in Table VIII is more involved than that of previous models, but you may wish to carry it through to convince yourself of the correctness of the following simple result:

$$\hat{q} = \frac{s_1}{s_1 + s_2} \qquad [15]$$

VIII. SUPERIORITY OF HETEROZYGOTES
($W_{Aa} = 1$ BY DEFINITION)

	AA	Aa	aa	$Total$
Proportion before selection	p^2	$2pq$	q^2	1
Fitness	$1 - s_1$	1	$1 - s_2$	
Proportion after selection	$p^2(1 - s_1)$	$2pq$	$q^2(1 - s_2)$	$1 - p^2s_1 - q^2s_2$

PROBLEM. A certain allele appears to be holding steady in an isolated population at a frequency of 10 percent, despite the fact that only half as many of its homozygotes survive as do heterozygotes each generation. Develop a hypothesis to explain this phenomenon.

ANSWER. Since 0.1 is a value of $\hat{q}$ too high to be sustained by mutation pressure, the simplest explanation is heterozygote superiority over *both* homozygotes. We therefore construct the following hypothesis: that the heterozygote has the highest fitness, which means we assign to its fitness the value 1. It follows that the homozygote of the allele in question has a fitness of 0.5 and a selection coefficient (s_2) of $1 - 0.5 = 0.5$. Following the hypothesis through to its logical conclusion, we solve for s_1 using the equilibrium Equation 15 and obtain the value 0.056. The fitness of the homozygote of the other allele is predicted to be $1 - 0.056 = 0.944$, which is the equivalent of saying that the replacement rate of the homozygote of the other allele each generation is 94.4 percent that of the heterozygote. An attempt might be made to check this number in the field in order to test the validity of the hypothesis.

PROBLEM. A given pattern of variation is controlled by two alleles, a_1 and a_2. For every 100 offspring produced by a given number of a_1a_1 individuals, 200 offspring are produced by the same number of a_1a_2 individuals, and 50 offspring are produced by the same number of a_2a_2 individuals. Predict the ultimate gene frequencies.

ANSWER. By inspection we see that the heterozygotes have superior fitness over both homozygotes, and that neither allele will replace the other. We need to know the selection coefficient of the three diploid genotypes in order to estimate the equilibrium gene frequencies. To get the selection coefficients we first calculate the relative fitnesses, which are the ratios of the rates of increase (see Table III) to the increase rate of the most fit (the heterozygotes). These are

$$W_{a_1 a_1} = \frac{100}{200} = 0.5$$

$$W_{a_1 a_2} = \frac{200}{200} = 1$$

$$W_{a_2 a_2} = \frac{50}{200} = 0.25$$

Therefore the selection coefficient of $a_1 a_1$ (let us label it s_1) is $1 - 0.5 = 0.5$ and the selection coefficient of $a_2 a_2$ (labeled s_2) is $1 - 0.25 = 0.75$. The equilibrial frequency ($\hat{q}$) of a_2 is predicted to be

$$\frac{s_1}{s_1 + s_2} = \frac{0.5}{0.5 + 0.75} = 0.4$$

Now consider a real case of balanced polymorphism. The sickle-cell trait is a hereditary condition that is very common in human populations in Africa and parts of the Middle East. Controlled by a single allele (Hb^s), it causes red blood cells to assume a sickle-like shape when they are exposed to low oxygen tension outside the body. Biochemical studies have revealed that the trait is due ultimately to the substitution of one amino acid (valine) for another (glutamic acid) at one position among the chains of about 300 amino acids making up the hemoglobin molecule. So here we have genetic polymorphism of a kind especially amenable to treatment by the elementary population genetics models. Persons homozygous for "normal" hemoglobin ($Hb^A Hb^A$) of course do not show the trait. Heterozygotes ($Hb^A Hb^s$) show the trait in less than 1 percent of their red blood cells, and they feel no serious ill effects. Homozygotes ($Hb^s Hb^s$) display the trait in a large percentage of their red blood cells, and they suffer from a severe anemia (sickle-cell anemia) that usually proves fatal in childhood. In other words, the homozygote fitness is close to zero and the selection coefficient close to unity. How can such an unfavorable gene be maintained at high levels? It turns out that the frequency of Hb^s in different populations is correlated with the amount of malaria in the populations. Experiments with volunteers who allowed themselves to be infected with malaria (the variety caused by *Plasmodium falciparum*) demonstrated that heterozygotes ($Hb^A Hb^s$) are decidedly more resistant to the malaria than are the "normal" homozygotes ($Hb^A Hb^A$). Thus it would appear that one of the conditions required for balanced polymorphism exists in this case: In malarial regions, the heterozygotes have superior fitness over the normal homozygotes because of their greater resistance to this disease, while at the same time they are also more fit than the sickle-cell homozygotes because they do not develop sickle-cell anemia.

PROBLEM. In Yemen the frequency (q_s) of the sickle-cell gene (Hb^s) is 0.12. What does this fact suggest about the incidence of malaria in that country?

ANSWER. This single datum indicates that malaria of a dangerous variety is very common in that country. To begin with, q_s^2 ($= 0.014$) of the newborn children are destined to be afflicted with anemia, and most will die at an early age from it. In order to maintain q_s at such a high level, this attrition must be offset by a significant percentage of malarial deaths among the "normal" homozygotes. How great is this second mortality factor? We can make a rough estimate by making $s = 1$ for Hb^sHb^s, by assuming (quite reasonably) that the frequency of the Hb^s allele is at equilibrium, in other words that $\hat{q}_s = 0.12$, and finally by applying the equilibrium formula to solve for s_1, the selection coefficient of the normal homozygotes Hb^AHb^A.

$$\hat{q}_s = \frac{s_1}{s_1 + s_2}$$

$$0.12 = \frac{s_1}{s_1 + 1}$$

$$s_1 = 0.14$$

Thus following the balanced polymorphism hypothesis through to its logical conclusion, we predict that the fitness of the normal homozygotes (Hb^AHb^A) is $1 - 0.14 = 0.86$ relative to the heterozygotes (Hb^AHb^s). The hypothesis of malarial resistance leads us to conclude that because of differences in degrees of resistance, about 86 children are contributed each generation by persons born as normal homozygotes for every 100 children contributed by persons born as heterozygotes. Again, this is the kind of prediction that might be tested by careful field studies as part of an effort to improve our understanding of the sickle-cell phenomenon.

GENETIC LOAD

The amount of selection that occurs in an entire population is often referred to as the GENETIC LOAD, which is formally defined in the following way in terms of reduced fitness:

$$\frac{W_{max} - \overline{W}}{W_{max}}$$

where W_{max} is the fitness of the best genotype and $\overline{W}$ is the average fitness of the entire population. When H. J. Muller introduced the idea of the genetic load in 1950, it was an emotionally charged issue. Muller was concerned especially with the mutations caused in human beings by radiation. When such a mutation occurs, it almost always confers a lower fitness, at least in the homozygous condition. It will therefore be eliminated or at least held at low levels within the population. In other words, it contributes to the genetic load. The price for such a load in human terms is what troubled Muller and still should concern us all. For the lower fitnesses of the mutations are too often produced by hereditary diseases that cripple and prematurely kill their carriers. Nevertheless, we should keep in mind that this is only part of the story. The genetic load is also based on differences that do not harm the carriers in overt, physical ways. If one genotype produces an average of three offspring per generation while other genotypes produce only two, this contributes enormously to the genetic load of the population. The same will be true if one genotype is, say, twice as likely to take advantage of newly opened habitats as the other genotypes.

The concept of the genetic load has produced some curious dilemmas in evolutionary thinking. We will now consider one of the most recent and significant, which you may be able to solve yourself. R. C. Lewontin and J. L. Hubby directly estimated the total numbers and frequencies of alleles in randomly chosen loci in a natural population (*Genetics,* 54: 595–609; 1966). They were able to accomplish this in *Drosophila pseudoobscura* by detecting slight differences in the electric charges of proteins. When mutations occur they produce their effects by altering the structure (and charge) of proteins. Even very small alterations can be detected by the technique of high-resolution electrophoresis, in which the proteins are allowed to separate in a strong electric field and then stained to pinpoint their location. Using this technique, Lewontin and Hubby discovered that about 30 percent of all loci in a single population have two or more alleles maintained in a polymorphic state; and individuals in the population are heterozygous for about 12 percent of its loci. These high frequencies were not expected. Lewontin and Hubby pointed out that they seem to impose an intolerable genetic load on the population. Each polymorphic locus requires stabilizing selection if it is to be maintained in a polymorphic state (recall the sickle-cell case). Thirty percent of the loci in *Drosophila pseudoobscura* means, by conservative estimate, at the very least 2,000 loci. How can enough selection occur to keep 2,000 loci polymorphic? Consider the following model to see how these numbers create a dilemma. Assume for purposes of illustration that the alleles have equal frequencies, and suppose that this balance is maintained by removing 10 percent of the homozygotes at each locus each generation. The reduced fitness per locus (the "genetic load" per locus) would therefore be

$$\frac{W_{max} - \overline{W}}{W_{max}} = \frac{1 - (0.5 \times 0.9 + 0.5 \times 1)}{1} = 0.05$$

If there are 2,000 such polymorphic loci, the relative population fitness would seem to be reduced to

$$(0.95)^{2,000} = 10^{-46}$$

Virtually all other reasonable numbers for homozygote fitness and allele frequencies put into this model give similarly impossible genetic loads. For example, if only 2% of the homozygotes are eliminated, the fitness would still be cut to 10^{-9}. The population would have to go extinct many times over to achieve such a level of polymorphism!

PROBLEM. Lewontin and Hubby could at first see no way out of the dilemma of the excessive genetic load, but a relatively simple solution does present itself if one thinks about the way selection works on the phenotypes of entire organisms rather than on the separate loci. Can you see the answer?

ANSWER. No fewer than three geneticists independently suggested the following solution. The difficulty stems from treating each locus as though it were subject to selection separate from the others, and then summing thousands of selective processes as though they were independent events. But the individual is the unit of selection, not the locus. The environment acts upon the total finished phenotype rather than upon the loci separately. It is reasonable to assume that the alleles at different loci interact in favorable or unfavorable ways to produce the final product. Many, in fact, contribute in a cumulative manner to the very same character. As a consequence, alleles are more likely to be tested as members of groups rather than as isolated units. Under this condition the total cost of maintaining loci in polymorphic states could be (and must be) far lower than envisaged in the original model.

EVOLUTION IN A HETEROGENEOUS ENVIRONMENT

To speak of the selection coefficient (s) as a constant is the same as saying that the environment is unchanging. Of course neither statement is correct. The environment is heterogeneous in space and time. A short flight can carry a bird from forest to field; a 180° walk of but a centimeter can take an insect from the hot sunshine on the upper surface of a leaf to the cool shade of its lower surface. The physical environment changes rhythmically through each day and season and, as an outcome of ordinary climatic fluctuation, in unpredictable patterns from year to year. The biotic environment also changes: the species on which a population feeds, or for which it serves as prey or competitor, shift in composition and relative abundance through space and time.

The study of population genetics in fluctuating environments is currently in its earliest stages of exploration. Here we will provide a limited introduction to one recent theoretical approach invented by Richard Levins. Levins' concept of the FITNESS SET is important not just because it attempts to deal with the environment in a more realistic way, but also because the method of analysis represents a radical departure from the classical population genetics you have been learning to this point. At the very least the serious student will want to know about this alternative approach to the subject, even if he is not yet prepared to pursue the rather difficult, advanced (and largely untested) aspects of the theory.

First look at Figure 10. Here we are concerned with the

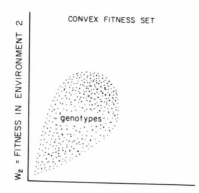
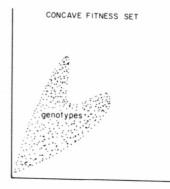

W₂ = FITNESS IN ENVIRONMENT 2

CONVEX FITNESS SET

genotypes

CONCAVE FITNESS SET

genotypes

W₁ = FITNESS IN ENVIRONMENT 1

10 FITNESS SETS in heterogeneous environments. Each dot represents a different genotype. Its position with reference to each axis represents the fitness in the particular environment represented by that axis.

fitness of different genotypes (each one represented by a dot) in two kinds of local habitats occupied by the population. Suppose the species we are considering is an insect and the two habitats are oak trees and fir trees mixed together in a natural woodland. The fitness of an insect genotype in an oak tree is denoted W_1 and measured along the horizontal axis, and the fitness of the genotype in a fir tree is denoted W_2 and measured along the vertical axis. Then each genotype can be represented as a point in the two-dimensional display of fitnesses in the two habitats. Notice that the patterns formed by the points can vary greatly. They can, for example, assume convex or concave shapes as exemplified in Figure 10. Now look at Figure 11. Suppose that at the locality we selected (call it locality A) some proportion p_A of the trees are oak trees and the remaining proportion q_A of the trees are fir trees. The average fitness at locality A of any given genotype ($\overline{W}$) is therefore

$$\overline{W} = p_A W_1 + q_A W_2 \qquad [16]$$

In this formula p_A and q_A are constants and W_1 and W_2 depend on the particular genotype chosen. Now the problem can be phrased in the traditional Darwinian terms: Which genotype is the most fit? This is the genotype that will prevail at locality A. The straight line labeled A in Figure 11 is the curve based on Equation 16 but rewritten in the form

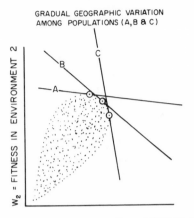
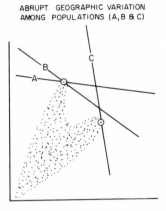

GRADUAL GEOGRAPHIC VARIATION AMONG POPULATIONS (A, B & C)

ABRUPT GEOGRAPHIC VARIATION AMONG POPULATIONS (A, B & C)

W_2 = FITNESS IN ENVIRONMENT 2

W_1 = FITNESS IN ENVIRONMENT 1

11   EFFECT OF VARYING the shape of the fitness sets among geographically separate populations *A*, *B*, and *C*. Figure on the left shows how gradual geographic variation arises from convex fitness sets; the figure on the right shows how abrupt geographic variation arises from concave fitness sets.

$$W_2 = \frac{\overline{W}}{q_A} - \frac{p_A}{q_A} W_1$$

Notice that p_A and q_A are constants, and that if we assign some fixed value to $\overline{W}$, the relation between the variables W_1 and W_2 is expressed in the graph as a straight line. For each value of $\overline{W}$ chosen, a different line is obtained—in a different position but with the same slope. We are interested, however, in only one member of this family of curves: The one that touches a genotype in the population and yields the highest possible value of $\overline{W}$. This is the line labeled *A* in Figure 11. You can see that given a final slope (fixed because the relative frequencies of oak and fir trees at locality *A* are constant) there is one outermost point touched by the family of *A*-lines. You can also see that this genotype has the highest combined fitness W_1 and W_2 of all the genotypes, and it will be favored at locality *A* by natural selection.

Now let us move on to locality *B*, where oak and fir trees occur in different proportions; call these proportions p_B and q_B. The slope of the $\overline{W}$ curves at locality *B* therefore differs from that at locality *A*, as shown in Figure 11. In the convex fitness set, the favored genotype at *B* is different from that at *A*. At the third locality, C, the outcome is different again; and so on. If this change through space of the proportion of oak and fir trees is gradual, in other words if the important aspect of the environment is heterogeneous in a regular way, the outcome will be a regular form of geographic variation within the species. The outward result might be a tendency for larger individuals, or darker individuals, or whatever, to prevail as one moves into parts of the range increasingly dominated by one kind of tree over the other. Of course this result can be generalized to other kinds of habitats, and to more than two coexisting habitats.

In contrast to gradual geographic variation, the concave fitness set can produce abrupt transitions in genotypes as we pass from one population to the next. By studying the analysis provided on the right side of Figure 11, it should become quickly apparent why this is so. A great deal of change can occur in the proportion of the habitats (and hence in the slopes of the fitness curves) without changing the identity of the favored genotype. Then, at a certain point, a little change in the proportion causes the fitness curve to touch a genotype on the other side of the fitness set. A strong character change in the species might be the outward result. Notice that the proportions of oaks and firs could be changing in space in an identical fashion to that envisaged in the convex fitness set. However, the effect this change in environment has on geographic variation is radically different. The shape of the convex fitness set produces a gradual change in the species through space, while that of the concave set allows no change for a while and then causes a considerable change in the midst of a gradually changing environment. Taxonomists are familiar with both kinds of pattern in their studies of SUBSPECIES (geographic races belonging to the same species). In some cases a gradually changing environment is associated with a CLINE, or gradual geographic variation in some character. In other cases it is associated with abrupt changes in the character; the "subspecies" borders, in other words, are more sharply demarcated.

A couple of qualifications must now be attached to this quite theoretical topic. The graphs of Figures 10 and 11 are products of the imagination. Fitness sets and fitness curves have not yet been adequately exemplified in field and laboratory studies. Fitness set theory is not the only way to account for differences in patterns of geographic variation. In most instances one can still provide adequate theoretical explanations by use of classical population genetics. The reason for becoming acquainted with the idea is that in some ways it provides a more flexible and general approach that allows us to think more clearly about the complexities of evolution in a changing environment. It also provides the possibility for some novel forms of research. How, for example, could the two kinds of fitness sets come into existence? Fitness sets of one sort or another certainly exist, but why are they not all convex or all concave? One can expect convex sets to exist when the genotypes are able to adapt physiologically and behaviorally to different environments. In other words, if each genotype is able to adjust to oak trees about as well as to fir trees, the fitness of each will not differ greatly in the two environments, and a convex fitness set will result. If, however, each genotype is not very flexible, and it is therefore usually much more adaptive in one habitat than in the other, a concave fitness set will be produced. Thus the more pronounced the influence of heredity in predestining this genotype or that for life in one or the other habitats, regardless of where the organism actually ends up dwelling, the more likely it is that the fitness set will assume a concave shape.

HERITABILITY AND POLYGENIC INHERITANCE

The elementary stages of classical theory were concerned with systems of inheritance based on pairs of alleles situated on the same locus. We know, however, that most phenotypic traits are controlled by POLYGENES, ensembles of genes located on two or more loci. How can this fundamental aspect of genetics be taken into account in evolutionary theory? Geneticists do attempt to analyze polygenic systems by construction of models based on the first principles with which you are now familiar. It is easy to see why the subject has grown complex and rather esoteric, with a heavy reliance on special mathematical techniques and computer simulations. Nevertheless, there is no reason why the interested student cannot proceed directly from the *Primer* into this more advanced subject with the assistance of more advanced texts such as those by Li (1955), Lerner (1958), Falconer (1960), Wallace (1968), and Crow and Kimura (1970). In the meantime the following account will provide you with some of the basic ideas.

Earlier, the concept of heritability was mentioned. The greater the heritability of a given characteristic, that is, the more its variation among individuals of the same population is due to heredity, the more rapidly it will evolve in the population under the influence of a given intensity of selection. Of course this fact alone is of paramount interest to agricultural scientists who prescribe techniques in plant and animal breeding, and that is why they have made important contributions to the study of polygenic inheritance as a byproduct of their work (see Lerner, 1958). In simplest terms, heritability is a precise measure that compares the total amount of phenotypic variability with the amount due strictly to the variation in genes. It can be estimated as follows. The total PHENOTYPIC VARIANCE (V_P) of a trait is the dispersion in the entire population of the trait, where dispersion is given precise form as the variance—a statistic that can be obtained directly from measurements of the population (see Chapter 1). The phenotypic variance is the sum of the GENETIC VARIANCE (V_G) and ENVIRONMENTAL VARIANCE (V_E). The genetic variance in turn is the variance due to differences among genes affecting the trait, and the environmental variance is the variance due to differing environments as they affect individual development. HERITABILITY IN THE BROAD SENSE (h_B^2) is the proportion that genetic variance contributes to the total phenotypic variance:

$$h_B^2 = \frac{V_G}{V_P} = \frac{V_G}{V_G + V_E}$$

A heritability score of 1 means that all of the variation in the population is due to the differences between genotypes, and no variation is caused in the same genotype by the influence of the environment. A score of 0 means that all of the variation is caused by the environment; in other words, genetic differences among individuals have no influence. Heritability is a very valuable concept but one that must be used with great care. Notice that its magnitude depends on the character selected for measurement. Different characters in the same population vary drastically in their heritability scores. Notice also that heritability depends on the environment in which the population lives. The same population, with an unchanged genetic constitution, can yield a different heritability score for a given characteristic if placed in a new environment. Furthermore, it is possible to dissect heritability into components, for the same reason that it is possible to dissect heredity (or environment) into distinct parts. For example, in the case of additive inheritance,

$$V_G = V_A + V_D + V_I$$

where

V_A is the variance due to the additive effect of genes contributing to the various individual genotypes. Some of the genes cause more of the characteristic (such as size, color, or bristle number) to develop, some less; and the sum of the effects of the combination of such genes assembled in each individual helps to determine the degree to which the characteristic develops. Variation due to different combinations of these additive genes is V_A.

V_D is the variance due to dominance deviations, i.e., differences in the degrees of dominance of given genes over others at the same locus.

V_I is the variance due to epistatic interactions, i.e., the various forms of suppression or enhancement among genes located at different loci. For example, the presence of b_1 at a given locus might suppress the contribution to the characteristic of a_1 on a second locus, whereas the presence of b_2 might not.

From the three components of genetic variance, it is possible to separate out a narrower measure of heritability that permits a direct estimate of the rate at which evolution can occur. This HERITABILITY IN THE NARROW SENSE (h_N^2) is defined as follows:

$$h_N^2 = \frac{V_A}{V_P}$$

The speed with which a trait is evolving in a population increases as the product of its heritability (in the narrow sense) and the intensity of the selection process. To be somewhat more precise, $R = h_N^2 S$, where R is the response of the population to selection, h_N^2 is heritability in the narrow sense, and S is a parameter determined in part by the proportion of the population included in the selection process.

THE FUNDAMENTAL THEOREM OF NATURAL SELECTION

The measure of heritability led us to the idea that the more a certain amount of phenotypic variation in a population is caused by variation in the underlying genes, the more rapidly evolution can occur within the scope of the variation. We now can state a more general relationship that was already sensed by Darwin, although in qualitative terms and without the benefit of modern genetics: the more genetic variation that exists, the more rapidly evolution will occur. *The Fundamental Theorem of Natural Selection* states this relationship in precise terms: THE RATE OF EVOLUTION IS PROPORTIONAL TO THE GENETIC VARIANCE OF THE POPULATION. It can also be shown that under certain simple but very reasonable conditions, the rate of evolution is exactly equal to sV, the gradient of selection pressure multiplied by the genetic variance. In other words, the rate of evolution is equal to the degree of selection pressure multiplied by the amount of genetic variation on which the selection is acting.

We will now derive this simple but basic theorem. A knowledge of integral calculus is useful but not essential for the understanding of the argument. For those unfamiliar with calculus, we will explain the notations as we go along. Consider first the case of dynamic selection illustrated in Figure 7, where the population evolves from left to right along some gradient of genotypes. The fitness increases gradually from left to right. We must refer the gradient of genotypes to the characteristic they control and upon which the selection is acting. In other words, we must label each genotype according to the average body length it causes, or the size of the food particle it most efficiently utilizes, or whatever the phenotype happens to be. But for our immediate purposes it will be useful to think as much as possible of the genotype and the fitness of each, while bearing in mind that each is associated with a particular phenotype.

From the frequency curve of the genotypes (shown in Figure 7), we can obtain the frequency distribution of the genotypes, which is just a statement of what percentage (i.e., frequency) of organisms in the population belongs to each genotype. And from the frequency distribution of the genotypes, we can obtain the mean and variance of the genotypes. These statistics are based on the direct measurements of the phenotypes, but then referred to the underlying genotypes. Suppose that there were 3 genotypes, equally abundant in a population of plants, that caused leaves to have 1 spot, 2 spots, and 3 spots respectively. Then the *mean* of the spot number in the population would be calculated as follows:

$$\text{Mean} = \frac{1 + 2 + 3}{3} = 2 \text{ spots}$$

The variance, which measures the degree of divergence away from the mean value by individuals in the population, is computed as follows:

$$\text{Variance} = \frac{(2 - 1)^2 + (2 - 2)^2 + (3 - 2)^2}{3} = \frac{2}{3}$$

Now suppose that 1-spotted, 2-spotted, and 3-spotted plants are not equally distributed in the population. Twenty-five percent (0.25) are 1-spotted, 50 percent (0.50) are 2-spotted, and 25 percent (0.25) are 3-spotted. The mean and variance are calculated by weighting each value according to those frequencies just cited:

Mean $= 0.25 \times 1 + 0.50 \times 2 + 0.25 \times 3 = 2$

Variance $= 0.25 \times (2-1)^2 + 0.50 \times (2-2)^2 + 0.25 \times (3-2)^2$

$$= \frac{1}{2}$$

In symbols, let x represent the number of spots (or any other phenotype controlled by a certain genotype). Let $g(x)$ represent the frequency of a given phenotype or its associated genotype; thus in the example above, $g(2) = 0.50$. Let $\bar{x}$ be the mean and V be the variance. Finally, consider the computations of $\bar{x}$ and V exemplified above, but this time for a great many genotypes that control variants of the evolving characteristic. The definitions given can be translated into the notation of integral calculus as follows:

$$\bar{x} = \int x g(x) dx \qquad \text{Mean}$$
$$V = \int (x - \bar{x})^2 g(x) dx \qquad \text{Variance}$$

The dx is used to denote the fact that the addition is occurring over a great many extremely small intervals of the phenotype x; in other words, we need not stick to gross classifications such as number of spots, or large versus small, but can measure phenotypes as finely as required to map the underlying genotypes.

Suppose that our population undergoes a selective event in which the chance of survival (or reproduction) increases linearly with the average phenotypic expression. If we refer all these fitnesses to that of the mean genotype (the one causing the phenotype $\bar{x}$), the fitness of each genotype x can be written as

$$W(x) = 1 - s(\bar{x} - x)$$

where $W(x)$ is the fitness of x and s is a number that measures the intensity of the selection (it is not the same as a selection coefficient, which gives the exact intensity of selection against one particular genotype). Note that the mean genotype $\bar{x}$ has a fitness of one by this definition, while genotypes having smaller or larger values of phenotypic expression have relative fitnesses less than one or greater than one respectively. (To avoid the possibility of negative values of $W(x)$, we must assume in addition that there are no genotypes more than $1/s$ units of x from the mean genotype or else that the fitness of all more deviant genotypes is zero.)

The selective event changes frequencies of each genotype to a new frequency, $g'(x)$, as follows:

$$g'(x) = W(x)g(x)$$
$$= (1 - s(\bar{x} - x))g(x)$$

Now we have finished making definitions and constructing the simple rules about selection. The Fundamental Theorem of Natural Selection can be proved by calculating the mean genotype x' of the population after the selective event. We will perform each step of this operation to show the algebra involved. Notice that basically nothing more than simple addition is involved, together with substitutions of terms based on the definitions previously given. In any case this derivation can be treated as an optional exercise not essential to the understanding of the Fundamental Theorem.

$$\bar{x}' = \int x g'(x)dx$$
$$= \int x(1 - s(\bar{x} - x))g(x)dx$$
$$= \int (x - s(\bar{x}x - x^2))g(x)dx$$
$$= \int x g(x)dx + s\int (x^2 - \bar{x}x)g(x)dx$$
$$= \int x g(x)dx + s\int x^2 g(x)dx - s\int \bar{x}x g(x)dx$$
$$\quad - s\int \bar{x}x g(x)dx + s\int \bar{x}x g(x)dx$$

(The last two terms can be added because they sum to zero; they permit the next step.)

$$\bar{x}' = \int x g(x)dx + s\int x^2 g(x)dx - 2s\int \bar{x}x g(x)dx + s\bar{x}\int x g(x)dx$$
$$= \int x g(x)dx + s\int x^2 g(x)dx - 2s\int \bar{x}x g(x)dx + s\bar{x}^2\int g(x)dx$$

(The sum $\int g(x)dx$ can be left in the last term after $\bar{x}^2$ is completely factored out, because it is the sum of all the frequencies and hence equal to 1.)

$$\bar{x}' = \int x g(x)dx + s\int (x^2 - 2\bar{x}x + \bar{x}^2)g(x)dx$$
$$= \int x g(x)dx + s\int (x - \bar{x})^2 g(x)dx$$
$$= \bar{x} + sV$$

By how much does the mean change because of the selective event? It is the difference between $\bar{x}$ and $\bar{x}'$.

$$\Delta\bar{x} = \bar{x}' - \bar{x}$$
$$= sV$$

Thus when the selection pressure increases linearly along the gradient of genotypes, the rate of evolutionary change in the population is equal to the product of the intensity of the selection pressure and the genotypic variance. Even when selection does not increase linearly, it can be shown that the evolutionary rate is in some way proportional to the genotypic variance. You will often see this more general relationship referred to as Fisher's

Fundamental Theorem of Natural Selection. In 1930 R. A. Fisher showed that the rate of increase in fitness is equal to the genic variance in fitness. What we have proved here, and labeled as the Fundamental Theorem of Natural Selection, is a similar but more useful principle. It is one that is intuitively more meaningful and can be applied more readily to actual observed cases of evolution.

GENETIC DRIFT

GENETIC DRIFT is the alteration of gene frequencies through sampling error. It operates to some degree in all finite populations but can probably be significant as an evolutionary force only in populations that are relatively very small. To gain an immediate intuitive understanding of what sampling error means, consider the following simple experiment in probability theory. Suppose that we were asked to take a random sample of 10 marbles from a very large bag containing exactly half black and half white marbles. Despite the $1:1$ ratio in the bag, we could not expect to draw exactly five white and five black marbles each time. In fact, we know from the binomial probability distribution that the probability of obtaining a perfect ratio is

$$\frac{10!}{5!5!} \left(\frac{1}{2}\right)^{10} = 0.246$$

On the other hand there is a small probability $[2(1/2)^{10} = 0.002]$ of drawing a sample of either all white or all black. This situation is analogous to sampling in a small population. In a two-allele Mendelian system, a stable population of N parental individuals produces a large number of gametes whose allelic frequencies closely reflect those of the parents; this gamete pool is comparable to the bag of marbles. From the pool, approximately $2N$ gametes are drawn to form the next generation of N individuals. If $2N$ is small enough, and if the sampling is not overly biased by operation of other forces such as selection, the proportions of A and a genes (comparable to the black and white marbles) can change considerably from generation to generation by sampling error alone.

Some amount of sampling error is inevitable in genetic experiments. We are accustomed to thinking of simple Mendelian experiments as producing fixed numbers; for instance, $3:1$ as the ratio of yellow versus green seed coat color in peas in Mendel's original experiment. Yet Mendel claimed that his experiment actually yielded 6,022 yellow and 2,001 green individuals. When the numbers from seven other confirmatory experiments published since 1866 are added, the ratio is 153,902:51,245 or 3.003:1. The ratio is not "statistically different" from 3:1 in the conventional sense, but due to sampling error, it is not identical with it either. Even in relatively large natural populations, therefore, it is at least conceivable that random processes play a minor role in altering gene frequencies.

In theory, three situations have been envisaged in which genetic drift might play an effective role in the evolution of small natural populations.

1. *Continuous drift*. The population remains small in size, and sampling error is effective each generation.

2. *Intermittent drift*. The population is occasionally reduced to a size small enough to allow drift to operate. Reduction can be effective in one or the other of two ways: (a) If mortality is random at the time of reduction, the sample of survivors can have a different genetic composition due to chance alone (the "bottleneck effect"); (b) if the populations remain small over at least two generations, the process of continuous drift is then initiated.

3. *The founder principle*. New populations are often started by small numbers of individuals, which carry only a fraction of the genetic variability of the parental population and hence differ from it. If chance operates in the selection of the founder individuals (and it almost certainly does to some extent), new populations will tend to differ from the parent population and from each other. The founder principle (or founder effect, as it has also been called) is of potential importance in the origin of species.

We will now state the way in which the effect of genetic drift can be roughly estimated. We are interested in the amount of change, Δq, in one generation in the frequency of some allele, a, due to chance alone. Since a statistical, rather than a deterministic process is involved, it is necessary to calculate the DISTRIBUTION of Δq in a large series of populations of the same size. If the distribution is truly random, the MEAN of Δq among the populations will be zero, since the sum of all Δq in the positive direction (gains in gene frequency) is equal in absolute value to the sum of all Δq in the negative direction (loss of gene frequencies). Each population has one Δq. When we sum up the Δq for all populations, the sum of the gains should equal the sum of the losses, yielding zero. What is interesting, then, is the dispersion of Δq among all the populations, measured by the variance. The distribution of q is binomial. The variance of a binomial sample about the mean q is pq/N, where N is the size of the sample. In the case of a Mendelian population, there are

N organisms formed from $2N$ gametes. The latter figure is the size of the sample, since we are dealing with $2N$ alleles with a probability p of A and a probability q of a. Therefore

$$\text{Variance of } \Delta q \text{ in one generation} = \frac{pq}{2N}$$

and

$$\text{Standard deviation of } \Delta q \text{ in one generation} = \sigma_{\Delta q} = \sqrt{\frac{pq}{2N}}$$

By the central limit theorem of probability, as N becomes large, Δq becomes normally distributed with mean 0 and standard deviation $\sigma_{\Delta q}$. Referring to tables of the normal distribution (also, see Figure 1–1), we find that two thirds of the time Δq will be less than $\sigma_{\Delta q}$ in magnitude, and only about once in several hundred trials will it be greater than 3 $\sigma_{\Delta q}$. Notice that these values are the MAXIMUM that can be expected to be due to genetic drift, since they are calculated from a model in which no other evolutionary factors are operating. In real populations, these other factors are usually, if not invariably, important, and they diminish the effects of genetic drift in proportion to their intensity. The model, therefore, gives us an estimation of the upper limit of evolution by genetic drift.

It should now be clear why genetic drift is an appropriate term for the process of random change in gene frequencies. Evolution by this means in any given population has no predictable direction; allowed to continue for several generations, the gene frequency would appear to drift about without approaching any particular value. The changes from one generation to the next follow what is called a RANDOM WALK in probability theory. The ultimate fate of any given allele is that it is either lost ($q = 0$) or fixed ($q = 1$), as shown in Figure 12.

The most important result of genetic drift is the loss of heterozygosity in the populations. Sewall Wright has deduced the following theorem: In the absence of any other evolutionary force (selection, mutation, migration, meiotic drive), fixation and loss each proceed at a rate of about $1/4 N$ per locus per generation. This function is useful in that it states the magnitude of rates of fixation and loss. The time to fixation or extinction of any given allele is therefore roughly $4N$ generations on the average.

What are "large" and "small" populations with reference to the potential of random fluctuation? Using the equations already given we can develop a preliminary intuitive idea.

1. *Small.* If N is on the order of 10 or 100, alleles can be lost

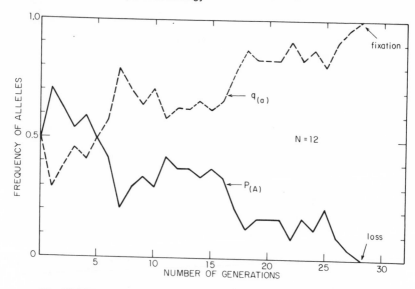

12 GENETIC DRIFT, simulated by the aid of a computer, led to fixation of *a* and loss of *A* in a population consisting of only 12 individuals. In general, the smaller the population, the more rapid will be the drift to these end points.

at a rate of about 0.1 or 0.01 per locus per generation. Also, $\sigma_{\Delta q}$ can be 0.1 or more of pq. Clearly, genetic drift is a factor of potential significance in populations of this size.

2. *Intermediate.* If N is on the order of 10,000, alleles can be lost at the most on the order of 10^{-4}/generation; $\sigma_{\Delta q}$ can be as high as 0.01 of pq. If allowed to operate freely, drift can force microevolution only to a moderate degree.

3. *Large.* When N is 100,000 or greater, the maximum potential gene loss is negligible, while $\sigma_{\Delta q}$ is now only about 0.001 of pq. A very slight sampling bias due to other evolutionary agents will practically cancel these modest effects.

In short, we would not expect genetic drift to be a factor of any importance in the present-day evolution of such dominant species as English sparrows and herring gulls, but it is conceivably critical for whooping cranes (1970 population: about 57) and North American ivory-bill woodpeckers (1970 population: under 20, if any at all). It has happened in the past that when the population of a vanishing species or subspecies, such as the European bison and North American heath hen, dropped to a few hundreds or tens of individuals, there was an apparent decrease in viability and fertility which hastened the decline. The effect has been attributed to the increase of deleterious genes through "inbreeding," i.e., genetic drift. The extinction rates of animal and plant species endemic to small islands are higher than those of related species on larger land masses. This "evolutionary trap" effect has been attributed in part to genetic drift, but other features common to insular endemics, namely small population size itself, together with a greater tendency to specialization, may be more important.

PROBLEM. In an isolated population containing 5000 breeding members, the frequency of an allele was observed to change from 0.50 to 0.45 in one generation. Could this have been due to genetic drift? To mutation pressure? To natural selection?

ANSWER. The quantity we need is a reasonable limit on the amount of change that could be due to chance alone, that is, due to genetic drift in the absence of all other factors. The standard deviation of the change in gene frequency under this condition would be

$$\sigma_{\Delta q} = \sqrt{\frac{pq}{2N}} = \sqrt{\frac{0.5 \times 0.5}{10,000}} = 0.005$$

In about 99.7 percent of all cases, the gene frequency would be expected to fall in the limits ($q \pm 3\sigma_{\Delta q} = 0.5 \pm 0.015$), or from 0.485 to 0.515. The probability that a frequency of 0.45 could be attained in one generation by chance alone is so small that the hypothesis can be safely discarded. This is not to say that genetic drift is not responsible for some of the change in gene frequency, only that it is extremely unlikely to be the cause of all of it. Turning to mutation pressure, we can with equal confidence dismiss the possibility of this factor causing all of the change. A shift from 0.50 to 0.45 would require a mutation rate of at least 0.1/locus/generation, which is extremely unlikely. Selection, on the other hand, can easily cause changes of this magnitude. If the allele were recessive, for example, and all the change were assumed to be due to selection,

$$\Delta q = -sq^2(1 - q)$$
$$-0.05 = -0.25(1 - 0.5)s$$
$$s = 0.4$$

This is a high value but well within the limit of selection coefficients that have been measured in real populations. It follows that the possibility of evolution through selection should be further investigated in this case.

THE SUBSTITUTION OF NEUTRAL GENES

In the last several years, population geneticists and biochemists have focused increasing attention on the possibility of evolution by the fixation of selectively neutral genes through genetic drift (see Crow and Kimura, 1970). The number of such genes with neither positive nor negative selective values must be small, and the chances of any one being fixed is even smaller. But given long enough periods of time, all neutral genes together might constitute a significant factor in evolution. Even when they have not yet achieved fixation, the neutral genes could contribute to the amount of genetic polymorphism in populations. How often is a neutral gene fixed in a population? The answer

turns out to be remarkably simple. The rate of fixation, measured in numbers of neutral genes being fixed per generation, is
equal to μ, the rate at which the neutral genes are appearing
at each locus each generation by mutation. This result is obtained as follows. If new mutant alleles are appearing at a rate
of μ per generation, then the number of NEW mutants present
throughout the whole diploid population in a given generation is
$2N\mu$. Once a particular mutant gene comes into being, it comprises exactly $1/2N$ of all the genes at its locus in the population.
Since it is neutral, it has the same chance as every other gene
present at the moment of its origin of having its descendants
fixed at some future date in all $2N$ positions in the population.
In other words, the chances that the descendants of a particular
neutral mutant will be fixed to the exclusion of all other genes
is $1/2N$. It follows that the probability that some neutral gene
that arose in a given generation will be fixed is the total number that arose $(2N\mu)$ times the probability that one in particular
will be fixed $(1/2N)$.

$$\text{Probability fixation} = 2N\mu \left(\frac{1}{2N} \right) = \mu$$

The probability of fixation is equivalent to the rate at which such
neutral genes are being fixed, measured in the proportion of
neutral genes being fixed per generation. Another way of viewing the process is to consider that the average interval between
the origination of successful neutral mutants is $1/\mu$.

Complete structural analyses of mammalian hemoglobins
have revealed that one amino acid substitution, reflecting the
fixation of a new codon, occurs at approximately the rate of one
substitution per codon per billion (10^9) years. This amount of
evolution, which is quite significant when all the hemoglobin
codons are considered together, can be accounted for entirely
by the fixation of neutral genes if these genes are originating at
a mutation rate of as little as 10^{-9} per codon per year. One in a
billion per year is an entirely feasible rate (see Table I). This is
not to say that hemoglobin evolution occurs wholly by genetic
drift. As you saw in the previous section, we can only "prove"
genetic drift by excluding the possibility of natural selection;
and the substitution of hemoglobin codons by natural selection
is still an untested possibility. What the result does demonstrate
is the possibility that all of the evolution might have occurred
by the random fixation of neutral genes.

Protein chemists have made the important discovery that not
only hemoglobin, but also certain other enzymes and biologically

active proteins, tend to evolve at a constant rate. For example, amino acids are being substituted in cytochrome C on the average of about once every 23,000,000 years. Thus there exist "protein clocks" that can be used to measure time in evolutionary lineages where the fossil record is not adequate for the same purpose. One might hope to obtain a more precise estimate, for example, of the times at which various protistan or invertebrate phyla originated in evolution. At present the data are inadequate to determine the accuracy of the protein clocks. Are they reliable to the nearest 100 million years? To the nearest 10 million years? If the phenomenon has been correctly interpreted, and can be calibrated with reasonable precision, it could provide a powerful new tool for evolutionary biology.

In the belief that the protein clocks are driven at least in part by the substitution of neutral genes through random drift, some biologists have spoken of the phenomenon as "non-Darwinian evolution" (see J. L. King and T. H. Jukes, *Science* 164:788–798; 1969). This does not imply, however, that protein clocks fall outside the domain of modern evolutionary theory. At most it means that a significant amount of evolution might have taken place without the guidance of natural selection.

Suggested Additional Reading

Crow, J. F. and M. Kimura. 1970. AN INTRODUCTION TO POPULATION GENETICS THEORY. Harper & Row, Publishers, Incorporated, New York. *xiv* + 591 pp. (The most concise and clearly written introduction to theoretical population genetics available.)

Dawson, P. S., and C. E. King, eds. 1971. READINGS IN POPULATION BIOLOGY. Prentice-Hall, Inc., Englewood Cliffs, New Jersey. (A very useful collection of research articles in both population genetics and ecology, for which the *Primer* serves as an adequate theoretical introduction.)

Dobzhansky, T. 1970. GENETICS OF THE EVOLUTIONARY PROCESS. Columbia University Press, New York. *ix* + 505 pp. (An authoritative review of research on the genetic basis of microevolution; strongly recommended reading for advanced students.)

Falconer, D. S. 1960. INTRODUCTION TO QUANTITATIVE GENETICS. The Ronald Press Company, New York. *ix* + 365 pp. (A very good introduction to classical population genetics, with more examples from experimental work than the comparable textbooks by Crow and Kimura and by Li.)

Ford, E. B. 1964. ECOLOGICAL GENETICS. Methuen & Co., Ltd., London.

xv + 335 pp. (A review of microevolution that is nicely comple-mentary to Dobzhansky's book because of its greater stress on ecology.)

Lerner, I. M. 1958. THE GENETIC BASIS OF SELECTION. John Wiley & Sons, Inc., New York. *xvi* + 298 pp. (A strong and clearly writ-ten introduction which lays stress on the principles of use in plant and animal breeding.)

Levins, R. 1968. EVOLUTION IN CHANGING ENVIRONMENTS. Princeton University Press, Princeton, N.J. *ix* + 120 pp. (This is the only comprehensive treatment of fitness set theory and related sub-jects but is difficult reading and can be recommended only to students with a strong mathematical background.)

Li, C. C. 1955. POPULATION GENETICS. University of Chicago Press, Chicago, Ill. *xi* + 366 pp. (A lucid presentation of the classical theory of population genetics.)

Mayr, E. 1970. POPULATIONS, SPECIES, AND EVOLUTION. Belknap Press of Harvard University Press. *xv* + 453 pp. (A wide-ranging and clearly written account of the origin and genetic structure of animal species.)

Sager, Ruth and F. J. Ryan. 1961. CELL HEREDITY. AN ANALYSIS OF THE MECHANISMS OF HEREDITY AT THE CELLULAR LEVEL. John Wiley & Sons, Inc., New York. *xi* + 411 pp.

Stern, C. 1960. PRINCIPLES OF HUMAN GENETICS. 2d ed. W. H. Free-man and Company, San Francisco. *x* + 753 pp. (Possibly the best general introduction to human genetics.)

Wallace, B. 1968. TOPICS IN POPULATION GENETICS. W. W. Norton & Company, Inc., New York. *x* + 481 pp. (A pleasant and clear review of a large part of both theoretical and experimental popu-lation genetics.)

Wright, S. 1968. EVOLUTION AND THE GENETICS OF POPULATIONS; VOL. I, GENETIC AND BIOMETRIC FOUNDATIONS. University of Chi-cago Press, Chicago, Ill. *vii* + 469 pp. (This and the second volume cited below constitute a treatise by one of the pioneers of population genetics and the "modern synthesis" of evolution-ary theory.)

Wright, S. 1969. EVOLUTION AND THE GENETICS OF POPULATIONS; VOL. II, THE THEORY OF GENE FREQUENCIES. University of Chicago Press, Chicago, Ill. 511 pp.

3 Ecology

THE POPULATION BASIS OF ECOLOGY

In this chapter we will consider some of the fundamental ideas of POPULATION ECOLOGY and COMMUNITY ECOLOGY—concerning, in essence, the growth and composition of populations and the ways in which these qualities affect other populations and are in turn affected by them. We will begin with the elementary equations that provide a quick intuitive grasp of the subject and the techniques for making rough estimates and descriptions of growth. Next we will proceed to DEMOGRAPHY, the analysis of the schedules of birth, of death, and of reproduction in the population. Demography provides the necessary information for obtaining a more exact measure of population growth, but it has other, far-reaching consequences in evolutionary biology that you will come to appreciate fully as you begin more advanced studies.

An understanding of population growth makes it possible to analyze the next level of complexity in ecology, the interaction of different species. Two broad categories of such interactions exist. The first is PREDATION, defined in the larger sense to include the eating of plants by animals and of animals by other animals. The sum of all predator-prey interactions in a given locality comprises the FOOD WEB of the locality. Knowledge of the food web, and of the rate and direction of energy flow through its many links, provides the means for understanding the efficiency of the system in terms of its utilization of energy. The system, incidentally, is called the ECOSYSTEM, because it consists of all of the organisms at the locality and their interactions with each other and with the physical environment. Information about energy utilization is required to measure and to interpret the stability of the ecosystem, meaning the duration through time of the individual species that comprise it and the degree to which the fluctuation in the numbers of organisms belonging to these species is kept under control. The second kind of species interaction with which we will be concerned is COM-PETITION, the striving together of species for whatever resources, such as food, shelter, or roosting space, that they encounter in short supply.

In the elementary theory with which we are concerned, the concepts will seem to flow one from the other with relative ease. To understand these concepts—and the often tangled controversies piled up around them—is to understand a large part of the core of modern ecology. But you should not be deceived into believing that ecology is founded on exact quantitative laws that serve to predict events with the same authority as the equations of, say, physics or physical chemistry. An ecosystem is vastly more complex than a gas-filled balloon or a flask of reagents. Proceed cautiously as you did with population genetics: Use the equations and problems principally to learn the ideas—to get the "feel" of the subject. In order to reflect the complexity of the systems actually found in nature, these basic ideas must be qualified and extended by techniques that are only beginning to be fashioned by ecologists. Often elaborate models must be constructed, and simulations of the real world performed with the aid of computers. We recommend that soon after you have mastered the *Primer*, you begin at least preliminary readings in more advanced textbooks, some of which are listed at the end of this chapter.

ELEMENTARY POPULATION GROWTH

Chapter 1 presented the elementary concepts of population growth chiefly as a device to illustrate model building. Let us now review these ideas and build upon them. The two simplest forms of population increase are exponential growth and logistic growth.

Exponential growth. Suppose that during a period in which population growth is observed, the rate of reproduction per individual remains constant. One female on the average, say, leaves two females in the next generation; two females leave four females; ten females leave twenty; and so on. In other words, if the rate at which individuals are reproducing is constant, then the rate at which the population as a whole increases is a simple multiple of the number of organisms already present in the population. The population with ten females breeds ten times faster than the population with one female, even though the rate *per female* is the same. This kind of population increase is generally referred to as exponential growth; sometimes you will also find it labeled geometric or logarithmic growth. Consider first the simplest variant of such growth. If, as in annual plants and many kinds of insects, the organisms breed only at one season and the generations do not overlap, the computation of the population increase becomes a relatively easy exercise. In the example just cited, each female leaves two females in the next generation on the average. And, if this is a sexually reproducing species, each male is replaced by two males. We have taken as the additional condition the complete replacement of each generation by the next. It follows that with each new generation the population doubles. If you start with ten individuals ready to breed, in the next generation you will have $2 \times 10 = 20$ individuals, the next generation after that $2 \times 2 \times 10 = 40$ individuals, and so on. To generalize, let R_0 be the net replacement rate per generation ($R_0 = 2$ in the example just given), let N be the population size (number of individuals in the breeding generation), let N_0 be that number at the beginning, and let t be the number of generations that elapse. Then

$$N = R_0^t N_0$$

Suppose $R_0 = 2$ as given, but we start with 1,000 individuals and watch them increase for five generations. The population size should then be

$$N = 2^5 \times 1000$$
$$= 32,000$$

Suppose, to take a second imaginary example, that you observed a population to increase its size by 50 percent in one generation. What size would you expect to have after three generations? In this case, $R_0 = 1.5$. After three generations the expected population size (if everything else stays constant!) would be

$$N = (1.5)^3 N_0$$
$$= 3.375 \, N_0$$

PROBLEM. A certain species of moth breeds in late summer and leaves only eggs to survive the winter. One local population of the species was observed to increase from 5,000 to 6,000 in one year. Predict the population size after two years, assuming no significant change in the environment.

ANSWER. The moth species is stated to be a seasonal breeder with nonoverlapping generations. Its rate of increase per generation, R_0, is $6{,}000/5{,}000 = 1.2$. After two years

$$N = (1.2)^2 \times 5000$$
$$= 7200$$

We will next consider the opposite extreme kind of exponential growth, that encountered in populations in which breeding goes on all the time. The equation which describes this process, you will note, can also be applied roughly to the case just reviewed, of seasonal breeding in nonoverlapping generations. The more generations involved, the more precisely the equation fits. For this reason, it is the most general of all growth equations:

$$\frac{dN}{dt} = rN$$
$$= (b_0 - d_0)N$$

where

$N =$ number of individuals in the population at given moment

$t = $ time, measured in whatever units are convenient

$r = $ a constant called the INTRINSIC RATE OF INCREASE, or the MALTHUSIAN PARAMETER; usually referred to in conversation as "little r" or just "r"; its value depends on the time units chosen

$b_0 = $ the individual birth rate, the number of offspring one individual will have on the average per unit of time; the subscript 0 indicates that this birth rate is measured when the population is very small (N is "near 0"), or else is growing rapidly as if it were very small

$d_0 = $ the individual death rate, the average number of deaths per individual per unit of time (if one in ten die in a day, for example, $d_0 = 0.1$ individuals per individual per day); again, the subscript 0 means that the death rate indicated is the one for populations at a very early stage of growth, or growing as rapidly as such very small populations.

This basic exponential growth equation states that dN/dt, the rate at which the population is increasing, defined as the number of individuals by which the population grows per unit time, is simply some constant multiplied against the number of individuals already present. That constant, the intrinsic rate of increase, is in turn the difference between the rates at which new individuals are being born, per individual, and at which previously existing individuals are dying, per individual. In other words, the model defines r as being equal to $b_0 - d_0$.

Notice that we do not claim that all population growth fits these rigid conditions. The parameter r differs from one environment to another. In a bad environment the individual death rate is higher and the birth rate is lower. In fact, d_0 can exceed b_0, with the result that r is then negative, and the size of the whole population declines exponentially. Also, the individual birth and death rates are never really constant through time even in the same environment. They change away from b_0 and d_0 as N changes, and in such a way that there usually exists some value of N at which they come to equal each other, so that N does not change any more. In spite of these shortcomings, there exist conditions wherein, for a time at least, the population grows AS IF the three quantities $r = b_0 - d_0$ were constant. This occurs when a population is well below the level that can be supported by the local environment. The elementary exponential growth equation can then be used to project population sizes during a limited number of generations for that particular place.

In doing so, it is useful to keep in mind one more distinction about the potential values r can take. Ecologists like to point out that, in theory at least, each population has an optimal environment—physically ideal, with abundant space and resources, free of predators and competitors, and so forth—in which its r would attain the maximum possible value. This value is sometimes referred to formally as r_{max}, the MAXIMUM INTRINSIC RATE OF INCREASE. Obviously, the REALIZED INTRINSIC RATES OF INCREASE actually achieved in the great majority of the less-than-perfect environments are well below r_{max}. For example, although the realized values of r of most human populations are very high, enough to create the current population explosion, they are still several times smaller than r_{max}, the value of r that would be attained if human beings made a maximum reproductive effort in a very favorable environment.

PROBLEM. In a rapidly expanding, continuously breeding population of human lice, r was calculated to be 0.111 per day. What is the rate of increase of a population of 100 lice?

ANSWER. The population size is increasing at the rate of $rN = 0.111 \times 100 = 11.1$ lice per day.

PROBLEM. Between 1700 and 1800 A.D. the human population grew steadily on a world-wide scale. It increased from approximately 600 millions to 900 millions of persons during that time. What was r?

ANSWER. The rate of increase, r, can be roughly calculated as

$$\frac{900,000,000 - 600,000,000}{600,000,000} \text{ per 100 years}$$

$$= \frac{0.5}{100} = 0.005 \text{ per year}$$

This estimate is actually a little high, because it does not take into account the fact that the population was growing continuously throughout every one of the 100 years. A more precise estimate ($r = 0.004$) can be obtained by utilizing the solution of the differential growth equation which will be presented shortly.

PROBLEM. By 1959 the human population had reached 2,907,000,000 and was growing even faster than in earlier times. On a world-wide basis, the birth rate was 36 per thousand persons per year and the death rate was 19 per thousand persons per year. What was the rate of population increase in 1959?

ANSWER. The individual birth rate (b_0) was $36/1000 = 0.036$ per year and the individual death rate (d_0) was $19/1000 = 0.019$ per year. The intrinsic rate of increase (r) was therefore approximately $0.036 - 0.019 = 0.017$ per year. The estimated annual rate of world-wide population increase in 1959 was

$$\frac{dN}{dt} = 0.017 \times 2,907,000,000$$

$$= 49,419,000 \text{ persons/year}$$

It is necessary to add here that r is subject to change in human populations, because the percentages in different age groups are changing. In particular, the recent spurt in the growth of humanity yields a higher proportion of young people, and hence a higher r, than would otherwise be the case. Only when the proportions of the various age groups are stabilized does r become constant. In fact, it is strictly correct to base the estimate of r only on stable age distributions, a topic we will explore more fully later in this chapter. Meanwhile, we must give the human r as being only approximately the number calculated from the raw birth and death rates; it is what demographers of human populations call the "crude rate of natural increase."

By "solving" the differential equation just presented (that is, $dN/dt = rN$), we can obtain a second, still more useful equation that allows the rapid projection of N through as long a period of time into the future, or past, as we desire. This growth equation is

$$N = N_0 e^{rt}$$

where N_0 is the number of organisms in the population at the moment we begin our observations (this can be any point in time chosen for convenience), t is the amount of time elapsed after the observations begin, and e is the constant $2.71828....$ Starting with N_0 organisms, we wish to know how many there will be (N) after t hours, weeks, years, or generations (or whatever units of time we choose) have elapsed.

PROBLEM. South America has one of the highest rates of human population growth in the world; $r = 0.023$ per year. In 1959, the population was about 137,000,000. Estimate what it will be in 1975.

ANSWER. The elapsed time t will have been 1975 − 1959 = 16 years.

$$N = N_0 e^{rt}$$
$$= 137{,}000{,}000 \times e^{(0.023 \times 16)}$$
$$= 198{,}000{,}000$$

to the nearest million. The value of e raised to a given power, in this case $e^{0.37}$, can be looked up in any handbook of mathematical tables.

PROBLEM. When Norway rats invade a new warehouse where living conditions are ideal, they multiply at a very rapid rate: $r = 0.0147$ per day. How many days are required for each doubling of the population size?

ANSWER. We wish to know how many days (t in the equation) are required to bring N to $2N_0$.

$$N = N_0 e^{rt}$$
$$= N_0 \times 2$$

It follows that $e^{rt} = 2$. We have been given $r = 0.0147$, and we wish to solve for t. Looking up $e^{rt} = 2$ in a table of exponential functions, we find that $rt = 0.693$. Then $t = 0.693/0.0147 = 47.14$ days. As long as the warehouse contains plenty of space and food, we can expect the population of rats to double about every 47 days.

Logistic growth. Population growth can obey the exponential equation only under special circumstances and for short periods of time. Any population miraculously permitted to grow at its full exponential rate for just a few years would come to weigh as much as the visible universe and to expand outward at close to the speed of light. Mankind, one of the slowest breeding of all organisms, might attain this level in about 5,000 years, if some power allowed us to continue multiplying at our present rate. Clearly, the exponential growth of mankind and a few other populations in which it has been recorded—usually under ideal laboratory conditions—is a very short-lived phenomenon.

Over long periods of time, in all populations of organisms, dN/dt averages zero or some value very close to zero. This is another way of saying that N, the population size, fluctuates up and down around some average value; every temporary increase in population is sooner or later canceled by a compensating decrease, and vice versa. The LOGISTIC GROWTH CURVE, illustrated in Figure 1, is a common (but not inevitable) curve by which exponentially growing populations approach their limit. This limit, the number of organisms (N) at which dN/dt is zero, is often called the CARRYING CAPACITY OF THE ENVIRONMENT, and it is symbolized by the letter K. By studying this figure you should be able to see why r and K are independent parameters. A rare species (low K) can have a high r; this simply means that it reaches its K faster. Conversely, an abundant species (high K) can have a low r, meaning only that it climbs to K more slowly. We will have more to say about the evolution and significance of r and K later in this chapter.

Now let us examine logistic growth more closely. The differential expression, stating the rate of growth, is called the LOGISTIC EQUATION (often designated more specifically as the Verhulst-Pearl logistic equation). It was derived in Chapter 1 as an exercise in model building (you should review that section now if you do not have it in mind) and takes the form:

$$\frac{dN}{dt} = rN\left(\frac{K-N}{K}\right)$$

which is merely the exponential equation, given earlier, multiplied by the term $(K - N)/K$. This latter term was concocted to express in the simplest possible manner the belief that as N increases, dN/dt decreases. When $N = K$, the term equals

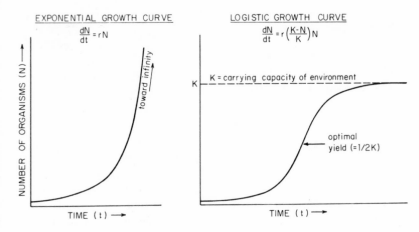

1. TWO ELEMENTARY FORMS of population increase: Exponential growth (*curve on left*) and logistic growth (*curve on right*).

zero, and $dN/dt = 0$. When N is close to zero, in other words when the population is just starting to fill up the environment, dN/dt comes very close to equaling rN; in other words the growth is nearly purely exponential. The term $(K - N)/K$ thus fits our intuitive idea of the simplest way in which a population could expand up to the equilibrium level, K. If N exceeds K, that is, if the population exceeds the capacity of the environment for it, this term becomes negative and N will approach K from above. In fact, any perturbation of the population size from K affects the rate of growth so as to return the population to its equilibrium size. K is what mathematicians call a stable, or persistent, equilibrium. The logistic equation is, to repeat, just a model, and undoubtedly oversimplified as a generalization, but it does give a reasonably good fit to many case histories of population growth observed in both the laboratory and the field. That is, many growth curves of populations allowed to start from the beginning are S-shaped ("sigmoid") and can be fitted to a logistic equation.

The logistic growth model contains several oversimplifications. One of the most serious is the notion incorporated in it that at extremely low values of N—indeed, when the population is on the verge of extinction—the growth rate is highest. But we know that populations at such low levels often are in several kinds of trouble. Mature individuals may have difficulty finding mates at the breeding season, for example, or inbreeding may cause increased homozygosity and loss of fertility. A more exact description may require that a lower limit be recognized below which population growth becomes negative and the population is doomed to extinction. The simplest way to express such a limit (let us call it M) is to add it as part of a new term to a modified logistic equation, as follows:

$$\frac{dN}{dt} = rN\left(\frac{K-N}{K}\right)\left(\frac{N-M}{N}\right)$$

In this equation the growth rate becomes negative, leading to the extinction of the population, if N is less than M; but it is positive for values of N greater than M. The new "threshold" term, $(N-M)/N$, is very important when N is close to the survival threshold M; but it is of minor importance while the population is large enough to exceed M by a factor of many times.

Why should populations be regulated in a way that yields a logistic curve? Abundant documentation exists in ecological journals to show that as population density, measured in number of individuals per unit area, goes up, there is a tendency for the individual birth rate (b) to decline (down from b_0) and the individual death rate (d) to increase (up from d_0). When b and d finally come to equal each other, the growth rate of the population (dN/dt) is, by definition, zero. This change in either b or d, or in both, is known as DENSITY DEPENDENCE. It is possible for b and d not to respond to changes in N (which in turn change the population density) over certain lower values of N; this would be DENSITY INDEPENDENCE (see Figure 2). However,

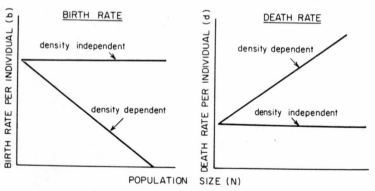

2   DENSITY DEPENDENCE and independence in individual birth rates (*left*) and individual death rates (*right*).

neither b nor d can be density independent over all possible values of N. At extremely high levels, both of these parameters are bound to be affected adversely from the point of view of the species—b downward and d upward. When d comes to equal b, the population stabilizes; the population has reached its equilibrium number K (Figure 3).

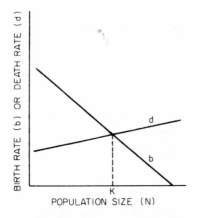

3 POPULATIONS STABILIZE (at $N = K$) when the individual birth rate (b) or individual death rate (d), or both, respond to the change in population density enough to make the two rates equal.

PROBLEM. From elementary propositions concerning the density dependence of b and d, derive the logistic growth equation.

ANSWER. This was the problem solved in the exercise on model building in Chapter 1. If you do not remember it, and cannot work out the problem on your own, refer back to this earlier treatment.

Ecologists often distinguish DENSITY DEPENDENT EFFECTS from DENSITY INDEPENDENT EFFECTS in the environment. A density dependent effect alters the birth rate or death rate as a function of the density of the population, and hence as a function of the population size N. Examples of factors that can have density dependent effects include competition among members of the population or between them and members of other species. They also include alteration of the chemical environment by secretions and metabolites, shortages of food, an increase (or decrease) in rates of attack by parasites and predators, emigration, and still others. In all instances, these factors by definition change in effectiveness as the population size grows. Sometimes the effects are positive. For example, a limited increase in density may help the population as a whole find food more efficiently and hence accelerate the rate of its increase. In most instances, however, the effects are negative. They tend to lower individual birth rates and to raise individual death rates. Long-range studies of natural populations have shown that in most cases density dependent effects play a decisive role in the regulation of population size. The particular factor or combination of factors involved varies from species to species. In one it may be mortality from parasites, in another shortage of food at certain seasons of the year, in still another an increasing tendency to emigrate, and so forth singly or in combination (see Table I). The factors also display the property of INTERCOMPENSATION, which means that if the environment changes to relieve the population of pressure from a previously prevailing effect, the population then increases until it reaches a level where a second effect takes over. For example, if the predators that normally keep a certain herbivore population in balance are removed, the population may increase to a point where food becomes critically short. If a superabundance of food is now supplied, the population may increase still further—until intense over-crowding triggers a disease epizootic.

Some events in the environment alter birth and death rates without having their impact influenced by population density; these are the so-called DENSITY INDEPENDENT EFFECTS. Imagine an island whose southern half is suddenly blanketed by ash from a volcanic eruption. All of the organisms on this part of the

I. THE OCCURRENCE AND NATURE OF
DENSITY DEPENDENT CONTROLS IN THE POPULATION GROWTH
OF EIGHT WELL-STUDIED INSECT SPECIES

(Based on Clark, L. R., P. W. Geier, R. D. Hughes, and R. F. Morris,
The Ecology of Insect Populations in Theory and Practice, Methuen, 1967.)

Species	Occurrence of density dependent controls	Nature of the controls
Codling moth (*Cydia pomonella*) introduced populations in Australia	Very frequent	Competition for feeding space among larvae and for cocooning sites among grown larvae
Grasshopper (*Phaulacridium vittatum*)	Very frequent	Primarily emigration; also (under extreme conditions) competition for food
Sawfly (*Perga affinus*)	Very frequent; weather also an occasional influence	In some regions, emigration coupled with competition; in other regions, parasitism by other insects
Cabbage aphid (*Brevicoryne brassicae*)	Very frequent	Primarily emigration (by special winged forms); also reduced fecundity
Sheep blowfly (*Lucilia cuprina*) in laboratory populations	Very frequent	Competition for food among adults, resulting in reduced fecundity
Larch budmoth (*Zeiraphera griseana*)	Very frequent	Hymenopterous parasites and granulosis virus, which alternate in prevalence
European spruce sawfly (*Diprion hercyniae*) introduced populations in Canada	Erratic; weather plays a major role in these unstable populations	Disease and insect parasitism
Psyllid (*Cardiaspina albitextura*)	Very frequent	At low densities, predation by birds and insect parasites; at high densities, competition for food

island, roughly 50 percent of the total from each population, are destroyed. Beyond doubt the volcanic eruption was a potent controlling factor, but its effect was density independent. It reduced all of the populations by 50 percent no matter what their densities at the time of the eruption.

An important theoretical consideration is that populations whose growth is governed exclusively by density independent effects probably are destined for relatively early extinction. The reason is that unless there are density dependent controls always acting to guide the population size toward K, the population size will randomly drift up and down. It may reach very high levels for a while, but eventually it will head down again. And if it has no density dependent controls to speed up its growth at lower levels while it is down, it will eventually hit zero. The density independent population is like a gambler playing against an infinitely powerful opponent, in this case the environment. The environment can never be beaten, at least not in such a way that the population insures its own immortality. But the population, being composed of a finite number of organisms, will itself eventually be beaten, i.e., reduced to extinction. For this reason biologists believe that most existing populations are under some form of density dependent controls that buffer them from extinction, and the empirical evidence (see Table I) seems to bear this opinion out.

Optimal yield. A second look at the logistic curve in Figure 1 will help introduce another useful concept of population biology: the OPTIMAL YIELD, or, to use more precise language, the MAXIMUM SUSTAINABLE YIELD. The optimal yield is the maximum rate of growth of the population under the conditions of the particular environment in which the population happens to live. It is also the greatest rate at which organisms can be removed without further reducing the population size—hence the expression "yield." Consider a population of fish in a pond. If you were an angler, or some more natural predator such as an otter, what would be the population size that produces the maximum number of fish each day for your diet? This is the "optimal yield problem" of ecologists. A study of Figure 1 should convince you that the solution of the problem is not simple. At K, when the largest possible number of fish is in the pond, there is no population growth and hence no yield. To remove some of the fish at this point is to drive the population size downward. Thus some lower population size must give the maximum yield. If the growth curve is purely and simply logistic, that point will be $K/2$, at half the saturation point. In Figure 1 it can be seen that when $N = K/2$ the shape of the growth curve is steepest; in other words, the rate of increase is the greatest.

PROBLEM. Prove analytically that in the case of pure logistic growth the optimal yield occurs when $N = K/2$. (This requires a knowledge of elementary calculus.)

ANSWER. To find the maximum growth rate, we differentiate the equation for the growth rate and set it equal to zero. The growth has already been given in its logistic form

$$\frac{dN}{dt} = rN \left(\frac{K - N}{K} \right) = rN \left(1 - \frac{N}{K} \right)$$

The derivative of this equation with respect to N is

$$\frac{d}{dN} \left(\frac{dN}{dt} \right) = r \left(1 - \frac{2N}{K} \right)$$

Setting the derivative equal to zero, we obtain the population size that provides the optimal yield

$$N = \frac{K}{2}$$

Of course, few populations obey simple logistic growth, especially when predation is occurring. Ecology is not that easy! Among the complications that enter into the picture is the fact that predators, including fishermen, seldom kill organisms of various ages with equal probability. Depending on the size and specialization of the predator species, either large, or medium, or small individuals are favored. This bias in mortality affects the age distribution of the population, which in turn affects r, the intrinsic rate of increase of the population. Thus, in solving the optimal yield problem, ecologists must include an analysis of demography, a subject we will review shortly.

r AND K SELECTION

The parameters r and K for a population in a particular environment are determined ultimately by the genetic composition of the population. As a consequence they are subject to evolution, in ways that have only recently begun to be carefully examined by biologists. Consider once again the logistic growth curve (Figure 1). Suppose that a species were adapted for life in a short-lived, unpredictable habitat, such as the grassy cover of new clearings in forests, or the mud surfaces of newly formed river bars. Such a species would succeed best if it could do three things well: (1) Discover the habitat quickly, (2) reproduce rapidly to use up the resources before other, competing species could exploit the habitat, and (3) disperse in search of other new habitats as the existing one began to grow unfavorable. Such a species, relying upon a high r to make use of ephemeral resources, is known as an "r strategist." The r strategy is to make full use of habitats which, because of their temporary nature, keep many of the populations at any given moment on the lower, ascending parts of the logistic growth curve. Under such extreme circumstances, genotypes in the population with high r would be consistently favored. Less advantage would accrue to genotypes that substituted an ability to compete in crowded circumstances (when $N = K$ or close to it) for the precious high r. The process is referred to as r SELECTION.

A "K strategist," in contrast, is a species that lives in a more stable, long-lived habitat—an old climax forest, for example, or the interior of a coral reef or a cave. Its populations, and those of the species with which it interacts, are consequently at or near their saturation level K. No longer is it very advantageous to have a high r. It is more important for genotypes to confer competitive ability, in particular the capacity to seize and to hold a piece of the environment and to extract the energy produced by it. In higher plants this K SELECTION may result in larger individuals, such as shrubs or trees, with a capacity to crowd out the root systems and to deny sunlight to other plants that germinate close by. In animals K selection could result in increased specialization (to avoid interference with competitors) or an increased tendency to stake out and defend territories against members of the same species. All else being equal, these genotypes of K strategists will be favored that are able to maintain the densest populations at equilibrium. Genotypes less able to survive and reproduce under these long-term conditions of crowding will be eliminated.

Of course the two forms of selection cannot be mutually exclusive. In all cases r is subject to at least some evolutionary modification, upward or downward, while few species are so consistently prevented from approaching K that they would not be subject to some degree of K selection. But in many instances where extreme K selection occurs, resulting in a stable population of long-lived individuals, the result must be an evolutionary decrease in r. For a genotype, or a species, that lives in a stable habitat, there is no Darwinian advantage in making a heavy commitment to reproduction if the effort reduces the chance of individual survival. At the opposite extreme, it does pay to make a heavy reproductive effort, even at the cost of life, if the temporary availability of empty habitats guarantees that at least a few of one's offspring will find the resources they need in order to survive and to reproduce. Most of the r strategists' offspring are likely to perish during the dispersal phase, but some fraction are certain to find an empty habitat somewhere to renew the life cycle.

DEMOGRAPHY

The details of birth, growth, reproduction, and death of individuals in a population are the basic ingredients required for the study of many aspects of ecology and behavior. Consider the matter of population growth. So far we have dealt with the subject as though reproduction is continuous, and all life stages breed, or at least as though a constant proportion of the various life stages contribute to reproduction. In other words, we spoke as though demography does not matter. But of course, it is crucial. Two extreme imaginary examples will make this clear. Suppose that all of the N individuals in the population were too young to reproduce. For a time, then, $dN/dt = 0$. Only later, after a few generations of unrestrained growth, can the growth rate be approximated as $dN/dt = rN$. Now suppose that in a second population all the N individuals were too old to reproduce. Clearly, dN/dt is negative; it will always be negative; and in fact the population will soon become extinct. In order to gain a precise estimate of population growth, we need to know how long individual organisms live, the ages at which they reproduce, and the rates at which they reproduce.

Survivorship and fertility schedules. The vital demographic information is summarized in two separate schedules: The SURVIVORSHIP SCHEDULE, which gives the number of individuals surviving to each particular age, and the FERTILITY SCHEDULE, which gives the average number of daughters that will be produced by one female at each particular age. First consider survivorship. Let age be represented by x. The number surviving to a particular age x is recorded as the proportion or frequency (l_x) of organisms that survive from birth to age x, where the frequency ranges from 1.0 down to 0. Thus, if we measure time in years, and find that only 50 percent of the members of a certain population survive to the age of 1 year, then $l_1 = 0.5$. If only 10 percent survive to an age of 2 years, $l_2 = 0.1$; and so on. The process can be conveniently represented in *survivorship curves*. Figure 4 shows the three basic forms such curves can take. Curve I, which is approached by man in advanced civilizations and by carefully nurtured populations of plants and animals in the garden and laboratory, is generated when accidental mortality is kept to a minimum. Death comes to most members only when they reach the age of senescence. In survivorship of type II, the probability of death remains about the same at every age. That is, a fixed fraction of each age group is removed—by predators, or accidents, or whatever—in each unit of time. Type II survivorship, therefore, takes the form of negative exponential decay. When plotted on a semilog scale (l_x on logarithmic scale, x on normal scale), the curve is a straight line. Type III survivorship is the most common of all in nature. It occurs when large numbers of offspring, usually in the form of spores, seeds, or eggs, are produced and broadcast into the environment. The vast majority quickly perish; in other words, the survivorship curve plummets at an early age. Those organisms that do survive by taking root or by finding a safe place to colonize have a good chance of reaching maturity. Extreme r strategists tend to have type III curves, while extreme K strategists are more likely to have type I curves. Can you see why?

The fertility schedule consists of the age-specific birth rates; during each period of life the average number of female offspring born to each female is specified. To see how such a

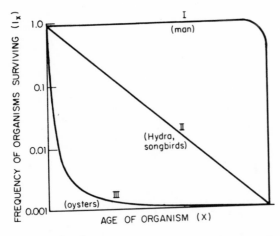

4   THREE BASIC TYPES of survivorship curves. The vertical axis is in logarithmic scale.

schedule is recorded, consider the following imaginary example: at birth no female has yet given birth ($m_0 = 0$); during the first year of life still no birth occurs ($m_1 = 0$); during the second year of her life the female gives birth on the average to 2 female offspring ($m_2 = 2$); during the third year of life she gives birth on the average to 4.5 female offspring ($m_3 = 4.5$); and so on through the entire life span. The fertility schedule can be represented even more precisely by a continuous *fertility curve*, an example of which is shown in Figure 5.

The net reproductive rate. The net reproductive rate, or replacement rate, symbolized by R_0, is the average number of female offspring produced by each female during her entire lifetime. It is a useful figure for computing population growth rates. In the case of species with discrete, nonoverlapping generations, R_0 is in fact the exact amount by which the population increases each generation. To obtain the net reproductive rate, one simply takes the fraction of females surviving to each age (l_x), multiplies it by the average number of female offspring produced per female at that age (m_x), and then sums up all of these $l_x m_x$ values for the entire life span. In symbols,

$$R_0 = \sum_{x=0}^{\infty} l_x m_x$$

which states that we should sum (Σ) the values of $l_x m_x$ ob-

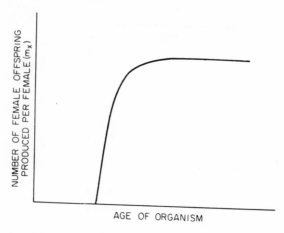

NUMBER OF FEMALE OFFSPRING PRODUCED PER FEMALE (m_x)

AGE OF ORGANISM

5   FERTILITY CURVE for human louse. This example is typical of organisms that reach sexual maturity at a definite age and remain fecund until death.

tained at each age x, for all ages from birth ($x = 0$) to infinity ($x = \infty$). Of course we will not need to count $l_x m_x$ up to $x = \infty$; after the maximum x that the organisms can live, in other words the maximum life span, all $l_x m_x$ are equal to zero, and we can stop counting. To see more explicitly how R_0 is computed, consider the following simple imaginary example. At birth all females survive ($l_0 = 1.0$) but of course have no offspring ($m_0 = 0$); hence $l_0 m_0 = 1.0 \times 0 = 0$. At the end of the first year 50 percent of the females still survive ($l_1 = 0.5$) and each gives birth on the average to 2 female offspring ($m_1 = 2$); hence $l_1 m_1 = 0.5 \times 2 = 1.0$. At the end of the second year 20 percent of the original females still survive ($l_2 = 0.2$), and each gives birth on the average at that time to 4 female offspring ($m_2 = 4$); hence $l_2 m_2 = 0.2 \times 4 = 0.8$. No females live into the third year ($l_3 = 0$; $l_3 m_3 = 0$). The net reproductive rate is the sum of all the $l_x m_x$ values just obtained:

$$R_0 = \sum_{x=0}^{\infty} l_x m_x$$

	$l_x m_x$ at birth ($x = 0$)		$l_x m_x$ 1st year ($x = 1$)		$l_x m_x$ 2nd year ($x = 2$)		$l_x m_x$ 3rd year ($x = 3$)
=	0	+	1.0	+	0.8	+	0

= 1.8

PROBLEM. In a certain population of mice 50 percent of the females survive to the breeding season each year, at which time they give birth to an average of six offspring equally divided according to sex. This continues to the end of their third breeding season, when the survivors all die of old age. Compute the net reproductive rate, R_0.

ANSWER. The information provided allows us to set up the following $l_x m_x$ table, from which R_0 is computed:

x (years)	l_x	m_x	$l_x m_x$
0	1.0	0	0
1	0.5	3	1.5
2	0.25	3	0.75
3	0.125	3	0.375
4	0	0	0
			$R_0 = 2.625$

Computing r from life-history data. We will now outline the method by which r, the intrinsic rate of increase, can be computed precisely from the survivorship and fecundity schedules. First, we will state the equation, which is easy to understand

and straightforward to use in practice. Then we will show how the equation is derived, a somewhat more difficult procedure but one that is necessary for a complete understanding of basic population ecology. The equation is the following:

$$\sum_{x=0}^{\infty} l_x m_x e^{-rx} = 1$$

You will recall that e is the base of natural logarithms; its value is 2.71828 and its various functions can be looked up in standard mathematical tables. The values of l_x and m_x for all ages x are obtained empirically, that is, by studying life histories of individuals directly. This leaves us with only one unknown, r, which we can proceed to solve. One of the simplest methods of solving for r is to substitute trial values of r until one is found that makes the left hand side of the equation equal to unity (that is, equal to 1.0, as shown in the equation). In more theoretical works, you will frequently encounter the same equation, which was derived by the eighteenth century mathematician Leonhard Euler and first used in ecology by A. J. Lotka, in the notation of integral calculus:

$$\int_0^{\infty} l_x m_x e^{-rx} dx = 1$$

This says the same thing as the previous summation equation, only more precisely. Instead of taking the intervals of time (x) in large units, such as days or years, the intervals are made infinitesimally small (that is, dx). Hence the value of r obtained will be very precise. However, in practice the first summation equation would ordinarily be used.

The Euler equation can be derived as follows. By definition, all of the organisms born alive are alive at the moment of their birth; in other words, $l_0 = 1.0$. We further note that the population is growing exponentially. It may also be standing still, or declining exponentially. In all three cases, the change in population size can be described by the elementary exponential equation, with r being either greater than zero, or equal to zero, or less than zero. We note finally that older organisms, probably of varying ages, contributed to the birth of our new organisms. Let us consider the parentage of the newborn organisms at some point in time, called t_0. For convenience let us make that moment right now. The parents born one unit of time ago, say a year ago, contribute m_1 female offspring for each female present. These one-year-old parents represent a fraction l_1 of the original group born a year ago. Therefore

II. DERIVATION OF THE EULER EQUATION
FOR POPULATION GROWTH WITH AGE-DEPENDENT
DEATH AND BIRTH RATES*

Time (x) previous to t_0	No. of individuals born at that time	No. of the individuals that survived to time t_0	No. of offspring born to the surviving individuals at time t_0 (by definition, these all sum to $l_0 = 1$)
$x = 0$	$l_0 = 1$	$l_0 = 1$	0
$x = 1$	$e^{-r \cdot 1} l_0 = e^{-r}$	$l_1 e^{-r}$	$l_1 m_1 e^{-r}$
$x = 2$	$e^{-r \cdot 2} l_0 = e^{-2r}$	$l_2 e^{-2r}$	$l_2 m_2 e^{-2r}$
$x = 3$	$e^{-r \cdot 3} l_0 = e^{-3r}$	$l_3 e^{-3r}$	$l_3 m_3 e^{-3r}$
.	.	.	.
.	.	.	.
.	.	.	SUMMED:

$$\sum_{x=0}^{\infty} l_x m_x e^{-rx} = l_0 = 1$$

Or, where the intervals of time are made infinitesimally small:

$$\int_0^{\infty} l_x m_x e^{-rx} dx = l_0 = 1$$

* We start at a given moment in time (t_0) and make the statement that all offspring are still alive at the moment of their birth $(l_0 = 1)$. The symbol $(\cdot)$ means a multiplication; thus $r \cdot 2$ means r multiplied by 2.

each female born a year ago contributes on the average $l_1 m_1$ female offspring at t_0. But notice that the population born a year ago may not have been the same size as the population born at t_0. How big was it? The present number of newborns, l_0, is the same as the number of newborns a year ago, l_1, multiplied by e^{rt}. Since $t = 1$ year,

$$l_0 = e^{rt} l_1 = e^r l_1$$

To obtain l_1 we divide both sides by e^r:

$$l_1 = e^{-r} l_0$$

The per-female contribution of offspring at t_0 by the individuals born two years ago is $l_2 m_2$. We get l_2 by following the same procedure used to get l_1. The only difference is that $t = 2$.

$$l_0 = e^{rt} l_2 = e^{r \cdot 2} l_2$$
$$l_2 = e^{-r \cdot 2} l_0$$

The dot ($\cdot$) between r and 2 above is a multiplication sign. The number of offspring born at t_0 is simply the contribution of offspring made by individuals born a year ago, plus the contribution by individuals born two years ago, plus the contribution by individuals born three years ago, and so on for all the age groups. In other words,

$$l_0 = 1 = l_1 m_1 e^{-r} + l_2 m_2 e^{-2r} + l_3 m_3 e^{-3r} + \ldots$$

Or, in shorthand,

$$\sum_{x=0}^{\infty} l_x m_x e^{-rx} = 1$$

This derivation is presented in slightly different form in Table II to make it still clearer.

PROBLEM. The calculation of r from most real life history tables is a very laborious process. We will give you a very simple imaginary example here to be sure you understand the basic procedure. The females of a certain insect species live only one year, at the end of which they give birth to 4 female offspring on the average. However, only 50 percent of those born survive to reproduction time. Calculate r.

ANSWER. We have only one row in the $l_x m_x$ table to consider. In this case $l_1 = 0.5$ and $m_1 = 4$.

$$l_1 m_1 e^{-r} = 1,$$
$$2e^{-r} = 1$$

Looking up $e^{-r} = 0.5$ in a table of exponential functions, we find $r = 0.69$. (Remember that this is the value of r only if we measure time in years.)

PROBLEM. Show the relation between the Euler growth equation and the formula for the net reproductive rate for the special case of a population that is neither increasing nor decreasing.

ANSWER. In a stationary population the net reproductive rate is unity; in symbols $R_0 = 1$. Also, $r = 0$. The Euler equation is therefore written

$$\sum_{x=0}^{\infty} l_x m_x e^{-0 \cdot x} = 1$$

which reduces to

$$\sum_{x=0}^{\infty} l_x m_x = 1$$

$$R_0 = 1$$

Reproductive value. How much is an individual worth, in terms of the number of offspring it is destined to contribute to the next generation? Another way of putting the question is: If we remove one individual, in particular one female, how many fewer individuals will there be in the next generation? The answer depends very much on the age of the individual. If we destroy an old organism, past its reproductive period, the loss will not be felt in the next generation unless it has been a contributing member of a social group. On the other hand, if we remove a young female just at the time she is ready to commence breeding, the effect on the next generation will probably be considerable. The standard measure of the contribution of an individual to the next generation is called the REPRODUCTIVE VALUE, symbolized by v_x, where the x in the subscript represents the age of the individual. The reproductive value is the relative number of female offspring that remain to be born to each female of age x. This value will usually be at its highest for females just at the age they start to reproduce, and for females beyond the age of reproduction it will normally be zero. As originally defined by R. A. Fisher, the reproductive value at age x (v_x) can be precisely estimated relative to the reproductive value at birth (v_0) by the following formula:

$$\frac{v_x}{v_0} = \frac{e^{rx}}{l_x} \sum_{y=x}^{\infty} e^{-ry} l_y m_y$$

Or, in the still more precise integral form

$$\frac{v_x}{v_0} = \frac{e^{rx}}{l_x} \int_{x}^{\infty} e^{-ry} l_y m_y \, dy$$

What is being summed in these formulas is the number of offspring that will be produced by a female from the age of x until the end of her life (denoted by ∞, or infinity, to be sure all females are included). The term y is used simply to label all the ages she will pass through from x to ∞. In practice v_0 is made equal to one, so that now the formula provides the reproductive value of v_x as a multiple of v_0:

$$\frac{v_x}{1} = v_x = \frac{e^{rx}}{l_x} \sum_{y=x}^{\infty} e^{-ry} l_y m_y$$

Thus $v_x = 2$ means that a female who has reached the age of x can be expected to produce twice as many female offspring as another female who has just been born. Why the difference? In this case, the high mortality of young females prior to reaching age x means that fewer will be able to participate in the reproductive process than those lucky enough to have reached age x. Suppose that for every 100 females born, only one reaches the age of x. This one female now gives birth to 100 female offspring. What is v_x? Since a female at age x is destined to give birth 100 times more offspring than the average female who has just been born, $v_x/v_0 = 100$. Setting $v_0 = 1$, we get $v_x = 100$, which is just another way of saying that the age difference makes a 100-fold difference in the reproductive value.

Now let us see how the Fisher formula for reproductive value is obtained. In words, v_x is defined as follows:

$$v_x = \frac{\text{the number of female offspring produced at this moment by females of age } x \text{ or older}}{\text{the number of females which are age } x \text{ at this moment}}$$

The numerator. The number of female offspring produced at this moment by females of age x or older can be calculated by modifying the Euler growth equation (see previous section) by considering only females who are x or older, instead of females of all ages. This modified formula is

$$\sum_{y=x}^{\infty} e^{-ry} l_y m_y$$

The denominator. The number of females of age x alive at this moment is the number of females born x units of time prior to this moment, in other words, e^{-rx}, multiplied by the fraction, l_x, who survive for the entire period of x. This product is

$$e^{-rx} l_x$$

Placing the terms in the numerator and denominator together, we obtain

$$v_x = \frac{\displaystyle\sum_{y=x}^{\infty} e^{-ry} l_y m_y}{e^{-rx} l_x}$$

$$= \frac{e^{rx}}{l_x} \sum_{y=x}^{\infty} e^{-ry} l_y m_y$$

An actual reproductive value curve for a population of human beings is shown in Figure 6. At this point make sure you fully

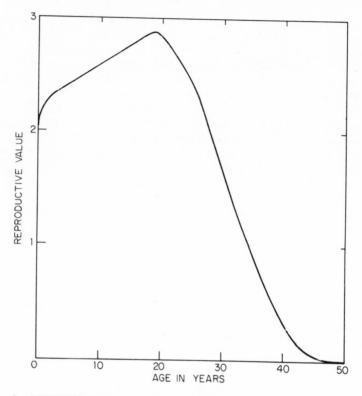

6   REPRODUCTIVE VALUES of Australian women in the year 1911.
(*From R. A. Fisher, The Genetical Theory of Natural Selection,
Clarendon Press, Oxford, 1930*).

understand why such a curve turns up and then dips down.
Notice, for example, the initial sharp increase immediately following birth. This increase is due to infant mortality. Do you
understand why?

The reproductive value has several important implications
for ecology and evolution. Consider first its relevance to the
concept of optimal yield. A predator, or a human farmer or
hunter, would want to do more than just try to keep the prey
population at about the level that provides the greatest growth
rate. Such a crude technique works only if the prey organisms
all have about the same reproductive value. A truly skillful
predator, or "prudent" predator as some ecologists like to call
it, would want to concentrate on the age groups with the lowest
reproductive values. By this means, it would obtain the largest
amount of protein with the least subtraction from the growth

of the exploited population. To take one example, dairy farms make use of the low reproductive value of eggs produced by continuously laying hens. To butcher the hens would be economically disastrous. At the opposite extreme, migratory salmon die shortly after returning to freshwater streams to spawn. In the few days between spawning and death their reproductive value is zero, and their large bodies form a rich source of energy for predators and parasites which can exploit them without subtracting from the growth of the salmon population. Is it possible that predators and parasites really evolve so as to select age groups with the least reproductive value? Wolf packs prey most heavily on animals that are very young, or very old, or ill—in other words, with the smallest reproductive values. But this may be mere coincidence; the same individuals are also the easiest to catch. The relation between predation and reproductive value is one which ecologists are just beginning to explore in a systematic fashion, and we cannot make any generalizations about it except the basic theoretical one given already.

A second ecological process in which reproductive value is a major factor is colonization. New populations, especially those that colonize islands and other remote habitats, often are started by a very few individuals. The fate of such a founder population is clearly dependent on the reproductive value of its members. If the colonists are all old individuals past the reproductive period, the population is doomed; because $m_x = 0$, and $v_x = 0$. If the propagules are all very young individuals unable to survive by themselves in the new environment, the population is still doomed; this time $l_x = 0$, and $v_x = 0$. Obviously the best colonists are individuals with the highest v_x. Is it possible that species that regularly colonize new habitats, in other words the r strategists, have dispersal stages with both high mobility and reproductive values? The evidence seems to favor this inference, although the relation of reproductive value to colonizing ability is still in an early stage of study. (Further aspects of colonization will be presented in Chapter 4.)

Finally, reproductive value plays an important role in evolution by natural selection. If a genetically less fit individual is removed from the population when it possesses a high reproductive value, its departure will have a relatively substantial influence on the evolution of the population. It is also true that genes which regularly cause mortality in individuals with high reproductive values will tend to be removed from the population more quickly than those that come into play at another age. It is in fact possible to account for the evolution of *senescence* by means of this concept. According to a hypothesis advanced by P. B. Medawar, senescence—that is, an increase in debility and mortality due to spontaneous physiological deterioration—is due to the fixation of genes that confer high fitness earlier in life but cause senescent degeneration later in life. If most of the members of a population are eliminated by predators, diseases, and other "accidental" causes prior to reaching the age at which the genes bring senescence, the genes will be fixed because of the increased fitness they confer when it counts. In other words, genes that add to fitness when the reproductive value is high and subtract from it later when the reproductive value is low, will tend to be fixed. When they are fixed, of course, they will in turn influence the $l_x m_x$ curve and, through it, the curve of reproductive values.

The stable age distribution. An important principle of ecology is that any population allowed to reproduce itself in a constant environment will attain a STABLE AGE DISTRIBUTION. (The only exception occurs in those species that reproduce synchronously at a single age.) This means that the proportions of individuals belonging to different age groups will maintain constant values for generation after generation. Suppose that upon making a census of a certain population, we found 40 percent of the individuals to be 0–1 year old, 50 percent to be 1–2 years old, and 10 percent to be 2 years old or older. If the population had existed for a long time previously in a steady environment, this is likely to be a stable age distribution. Future censuses will therefore yield about the same proportions. Stable age distributions are approached by any population in a steady environment, regardless of whether the population is increasing in size, decreasing, or holding steady. Each population has its own particular distribution for a given set of environmental conditions.

The best way to understand stable age distributions is simply to work one out. In Table III we have provided an imaginary life history table, designed to facilitate quick numerical operations. In the lower part of the same table is shown the numbers of individuals in each age group during six successive years. There are three age groups through which the organisms pass during a complete life span, and the number of organisms in the three age groups are labeled N_1, N_2, and N_3 respectively. In our example we arbitrarily started with a population consisting of 10 organisms in each of the three age groups ($N_1 = N_2 = N_3 = 10$), an array deliberately chosen to be far removed from the stable distribution. The point is that in the second year the l_x and m_x values will cause the proportions to shift. They will

III. HOW TO APPROXIMATE A STABLE AGE DISTRIBUTION
FROM LIFE HISTORY DATA*

THE LIFE HISTORY TABLE

	Age 1	Age 2	Age 3	Age 4
l_x	1	.5	.25	0
m_x	1	1	1	0

AGE DISTRIBUTIONS, STARTING ARBITRARILY WITH
10 INDIVIDUALS IN EACH AGE CLASS

Number of females in different age classes	First year	Second year	Third year	Fourth year	Fifth year	Sixth year
N_1	10	30	40	58	86	125
N_2	10	5	15	20	29	43
N_3	10	5	3	8	10	15
N_4	0	0	0	0	0	0
Total N each year	30	40	58	86	125	183

° The straight downward lines show the decrease in numbers of individuals due to mortality as the individuals grow older, while the dashed upward arrows indicate the combined contributions of new offspring each year for all age groups.

change in one direction until finally, after a half dozen generations or so, they no longer change to a significant degree—in other words they have approached the stable age distribution. We can start with any set of proportions of age groups we choose, but the population will always arrive at the same stable age distribution.

You already have the technique required to approximate a stable distribution. In the upper part of Table III, the l_x data tell how many individuals survive in going from one age group to another, and the m_x data tell the average number of female offspring each female produces each year. To speed the calculations we have made $m_x = 1$ in every case. Now, in the lower half of Table III, look at the shift in age composition from the first year to the second year. We start in the first year with 10 individuals in each of the three age groups (the fourth-year group is empty; it is included in the array as a row of zeros only to remind you that no individuals live into the fourth year). In the starting group, therefore, the age composition is 0.333 : 0.333 : 0.333 for the numbers of individuals in the three age groups. Half of the 10 in N_1, or 5 individuals, survive to make up the N_2 of the second year. Half of the 10 in N_2, or five individuals, survive to make up the N_3 of the second year. Notice that we get this last survivorship figure of one half from the fact that l_3 is given in the life history table as 0.25, while l_2 is given as 0.5; this means that half of the individuals who made it to year two make it to year three. Thus the figure $l_3 = 0.25$ comes from the fact that $0.5 \times 0.5 = 0.25$ make it all the way from birth to year three. Finally there are 30 individuals in N_1 in the second year because each of the 30 individuals alive in the first year gave birth to a single offspring. To get the age-class proportions in year 3, we merely go from those in year 2 by following the same procedure used to proceed from year 1 to year 2.

As we pass from one year to the next we find that the age composition changes each year, but to a lesser degree with each succeeding year. The composition is converging toward the stable age distribution. In the first year the proportions are 0.333 : 0.333 : 0.333. By the fifth year they have changed to 0.688 : 0.232 : 0.080. The following (sixth) year sees only a slight further change; the proportions are now 0.683 : 0.235 : 0.082. These last values are very close to the ultimate, stable age distribution.

PROBLEM. Individuals of an imaginary species of cockroach live a maximum of three months. Of those that hatch from the egg, 20 percent live to the second month and breed. Of these, 50 percent (or 10 percent of all the newborn roaches) live to the third month and breed. None live into the fourth month. Surviving female cockroaches produce an average of 10 female offspring in each of the two breeding months. A house is infested with 10 two-months-old and 20 three-months-old female cockroaches, all previously inseminated, who arrive uninvited in a piece of furniture from a contaminated warehouse. Describe the growth of the population and calculate the amount of time required to approach a stable age distribution.

ANSWER. The birth and death schedules and population history are given in Table IV. Because the age distribution of the founder population was so far from the stable distribution (in particular, there were no juveniles at all), the population size and age composition fluctuated drastically in the first several months. But by around the tenth month a stable age distribution had clearly been approached, and the population was growing at a steady rate. This case illustrates an important additional point concerning demographic studies that could not be adequately made in earlier sections: in order to obtain precise measures of the net reproductive rate (R_0) and the intrinsic rate of increase (r), it is necessary to observe a population which is at or near its stable age distribution.

PREDATION

For the purpose of formulating theory, ecologists define PREDATION in its broadest possible sense: The eating of live organisms, regardless of the identity of the organisms. Predation includes the consumption of plants by animals, called HERBIVORES, and the consumption of animals by other animals, called CARNIVORES. There are also a few plants, such as Venus'-fly-

IV. LIFE TABLE AND AGE DISTRIBUTIONS OBTAINED FROM THE DATA PRESENTED IN THE ACCOMPANYING PROBLEM

	Age 1	Age 2	Age 3	Age 4
l_x	1	0.2	0.1	0
m_x	0	10	10	0

							MONTH					
	1	2	3	4	5	6	7	8	9	10	11	12
N_1	0	300	50	600	400	1,250	1,400	2,900	4,050	7,200	11,000	18,450
N_2	10	0	60	10	120	80	250	280	580	810	1,440	2,200
N_3	20	5	0	30	5	60	40	125	140	290	405	720
Total N	30	305	110	640	525	1,390	1,690	3,305	4,770	8,300	12,845	21,370
Proportion of N_1	0	0.98	0.45	0.94	0.76	0.89	0.83	0.88	0.85	0.87	0.86	0.86

trap and the sundews, which capture and digest insects and are therefore carnivores. There exists a third class of organisms, especially well represented in the insects, called PARASITOIDS. Their behavior is intermediate between predation and parasitism. For a while the parasitoid lives in or upon the body of its living host in the manner of a true parasite, but in time it invariably kills the host by destroying too much of its tissues, in the manner of most predators. Because the host is killed (you could now correctly call it a prey), the ultimate result is the same as outright predation; and parasitoid and predatory behavior can be treated in exactly the same way in population models. In the literature you will often encounter references to "parasitism," especially insect parasitism, in the same context as predation in elementary model-building. But what the authors are usually talking about is the special case of parasitoid behavior. We do not wish to imply that true parasitism is fundamentally different from predation. However, because the host is often not killed in the end, the detrimental effects of the parasite are more subtle and not easily incorporated into models. The elementary theory about to be presented will be limited to straightforward predation.

The Lotka-Volterra equations. Predation is one of the truly fundamental processes of biology for several reasons: It provides most of the principal routes of energy flow through the ecosystem, it permits the evolution and build-up of many more plant and animal species in the ecosystem than would otherwise be possible, and it serves as a chief source of density dependent effects in the regulation of growth in a large percentage of plant and animal species. Let us begin by considering predation as a regulator of population growth. First we will examine the classical Lotka-Volterra equations of predator-prey interaction. Then we will see why, in the inevitable manner of a maturing science, the model on which the equations were based must be increased in complexity in order to bring our theory into closer alignment with reality.

The LOTKA-VOLTERRA EQUATIONS, so called because they were first independently proposed by Alfred J. Lotka (1925) and Vito Volterra (1926) during their pioneering research on theoretical population ecology, are based upon two very simple propositions: the birth rate of the predator will increase as the number of prey increases, while the death rate of the prey will increase as the number of predators increases. Let us label the predator as species 1 and the prey as species 2 and introduce the convention $2 \rightarrow 1$, which means that species 2 feeds energy into species 1, i.e., species 1 eats species 2.

The number of individuals in the predator population is labeled N_1 and the number in the prey population N_2. We start by recognizing that the individual birth rate of the predator depends upon the amount of food that is available, which in turn depends upon the density of the prey population. This is the same as saying that it equals B_1N_2, where N_2 is the number of individuals in the prey population and B_1 is a fitted constant. The individual death rate of the predator, on the other hand, is not so dependent on the prey; its simplest expression is D_1, which is also a constant. Putting these terms together in a modified form of the equation for exponential growth, we obtain

Predator Population Growth

$$\frac{dN_1}{dt} = (\text{individual birth date} - \text{individual death rate}) \times N_1$$

$$= (B_1N_2 - D_1)N_1$$

$$= B_1N_1N_2 - D_1N_1$$

This is the first of the Lotka-Volterra equations. The second describes population growth in the prey. The individual birth rate of the prey, unlike that of the predator, is not directly dependent on the abundance of the other species. Therefore we can describe it simply as B_2, a constant. The death rate, however, is directly proportional to the abundance of the predator and is most simply described as D_2N_1. These terms are put together to obtain the following equation:

Prey Population Growth

$$\frac{dN_2}{dt} = (\text{individual birth rate} - \text{individual death rate}) \times N_2$$

$$= (B_2 - D_2N_1)N_2$$

$$= B_2N_2 - D_2N_1N_2$$

The notion that the growth rates are dependent on the product of the numbers of organisms is closely similar to the principle of MASS ACTION in chemistry, namely that rates of reaction increase as the products of the concentration of the molecules involved in the reaction. Put in the simplest possible language, the rates of reaction depend directly on the rates at which the molecules bump into each other, which is a function of the product of the concentrations. By the same line of reasoning, prey get eaten by predators according to how often they bump into each other. Why is this the product of their numbers? Visualize the following idealized circumstance. Suppose that in a given area there lives one prey animal, which is quickly replaced by another if it dies. During a certain period of time, an average of one predator searches this whole area. Result: one predator-prey interaction. Now suppose two predators sweep the area in the same period, at different intervals so that the prey eaten by the first predator can be replaced by a second prey in time for the second predator to find it. Result: two predator-prey interactions. Now let there be three predators and three prey. Result: nine predator-prey interactions. By extending this thought experiment you can see more clearly the merit of incorporating products into the population models.

PROBLEM. According to the Lotka-Volterra equations, at what population sizes (N_1 and N_2) will the predator and prey populations be at equilibrium?

ANSWER. When populations cease changing, $dN/dt = 0$ by definition. Setting $dN_1/dt = 0$ for the predator population, we obtain $N_2 = D_1/B_1$. Setting $dN_2/dt = 0$ for the prey population, we obtain $N_1 = B_2/D_2$. Notice that these two equations generate straight lines in a graph of N_1 versus N_2.

After you have solved the above problem, look at the upper diagram in Figure 7. Notice that to the right of the vertical

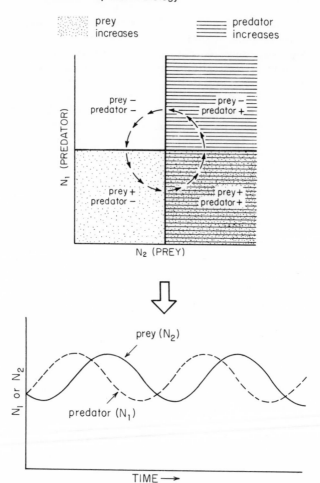

7 PREDATOR-PREY INTERACTION as predicted by the Lotka-Volterra equations. The upper graph shows the joint abundance of the two interacting populations. The lower graph shows the result when the abundances of the two species are plotted as a function of time.

line, which is the "curve" $N_2 = D_1/B_1$, the predator population is growing. It grows because when there are more than D_1/B_1 prey, the birth rate of the predator population exceeds its death rate. Left of this line the predator population decreases. Notice also that below the horizontal line, which is the "curve" $N_1 = B_2/D_2$, the prey population is growing; because now there are few enough predators (less than D_2/B_2 of them) so that the death rate of the prey population is less than its birth rate.

Next we switch to the graphical view of the predator-prey interaction. The arrows going around in a circle in the upper graph of Figure 7 represent the joint population sizes of the predator and prey as they change through time. Select a point on the circle of arrows somewhere in the upper left-hand quadrant. Since the point is left of the vertical line there are not enough prey to keep the predator growing; so the arrow is falling. And since the point is above the horizontal line, there are too many predators to allow the prey to increase; as a result the arrow is directed to the left. The point moves, therefore, downward and to the left. It will continue on this course until it crosses the horizontal line, at which time the predators will be scarce enough to allow the prey population to increase. Now the point on the circle of arrows moves downward and to the right. From here you should continue on around to complete the circle, seeing why it takes a particular direction in each quadrant.

Clearly both the predator and prey populations will oscillate up and down through time, as shown in the lower graph in Figure 7. In a perfect Lotka-Volterra system, the oscillations could form population cycles, meaning that the numbers of individuals would rise and fall repeatedly at regular intervals. Such cycles are known, and a few can even be interpreted to be at least roughly consistent with the Lotka-Volterra pattern (Figure 8).

However, we must add at once that predation is but one of several agents that can cause population cycles. Three other factors that have been implicated are mass emigration, physiological stress due to overcrowding, and genetic changes in the populations. Fluctuations are seldom regular enough to deserve the title of cycles. More often, they are highly irregular and very difficult to interpret.

Improvement of the basic theory. Population cycles are also very difficult to achieve in the laboratory. When predator and prey populations are confined together in simple aquaria or terraria the usual course of events is for the predator to eat the prey faster than the prey can reproduce, to search out every last individual, and thus to drive it to extinction. Deprived of food, the predator itself faces extinction. What, then, is wrong with the Lotka-Volterra equations? In a word, they are too simple. They generate errors in the set of joint abundances at which the predator and prey each ceases to increase. Without attempting to rewrite these equations, and recognizing in principle that the propositions behind them are basically true, let us proceed

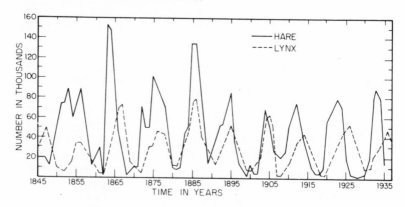

8 POPULATION CYCLES in the lynx and its principal prey, the snowshoe hare, in Canada. The vertical axis gives the number of pelts received by the Hudson Bay Company. (*From Odum*, 1971, *after D. A. MacLulich, 1937, University of Toronto Studies, Biology Series, No. 43*).

directly to an improvement of the theory in its graphical form. In other words, to use the language of the theoreticians, we will confine ourselves to graphical analysis and postpone the much more difficult analytic treatment based on equations.

It is in fact possible to account for a wide range of outcomes in the predator-prey system merely by making a couple of relatively minor and realistic changes in the zero-growth curve of the prey. Look at Figure 9. Now the prey zero-growth curve is drawn to be convex instead of just a straight line as dictated by the Lotka-Volterra equations. In our new version, the prey population can increase if the joint abundances of predator and prey (N_1 and N_2) fall inside this bulge; it decreases if the joint abundances fall outside the bulge. The direction of population change, indicated by the arrows, is judged in the same way as in the earlier, simpler graph based on the Lotka-Volterra equations. The diagrams in Figures 9 and 10 represent four different situations that could occur in nature. The first three are obtained merely by shifting the prey zero-growth curve relative to the predator zero-growth curve. In the first case (STABLE CYCLE) the predator zero growth curve intersects the prey curve at right angles, so that the two curves create four equal quadrants. Just as in the original Lotka-Volterra diagram (Figure 7), the arrows will tend to move along symmetric paths in each quadrant, creating stable population cycles. Such symmetry, however, must be rare in nature—just as regular predator-prey population cycles are rare. In the second case (DAMPED CYCLE), the prey zero-growth curve falls mostly outside the predator curve. The result, which can be intuited by examining the graph, is an

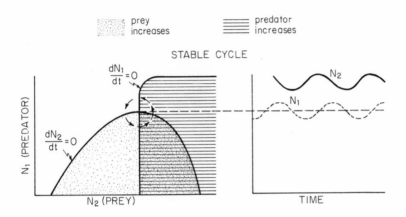

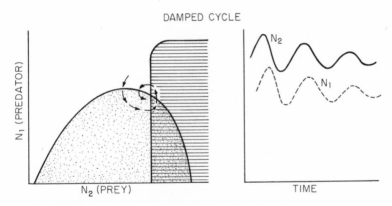

9   GROWTH CURVES of predator and prey populations. According to the theory, major changes in the predator-prey oscillations are obtained when the relative positions of the zero-growth curves are changed. The arrows indicate the directions followed by the joint abundances of the interacting populations. The left diagrams show the relationship of the predator and the prey in which each increases and decreases in long-range equilibrium. On the right, the relationships are shown as they change through time, producing the familiar population cycles. (*Redrawn from MacArthur and Connell, The Biology of Populations, John Wiley & Sons, New York, 1966, based on M. Rosenzweig and R. H. MacArthur, 1963.*)

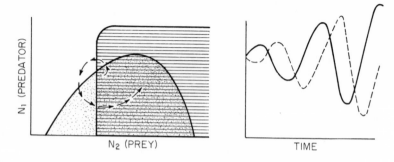

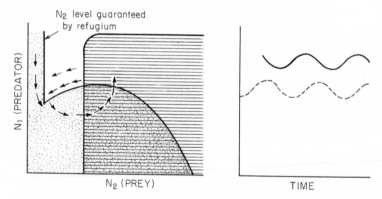

10   TWO ADDITIONAL KINDS of oscillations in predator-prey systems. (*Redrawn from MacArthur and Connell, 1966, based on M. Rosenzweig and R. H. MacArthur, 1963*).

inward spiraling path of arrows and a damping of the population cycles. The result would be considerable stability in the two populations. In the third case (UNSTABLE CYCLE) the prey curve lies mostly within the predator curve. This is the situation most likely to occur in simple systems, such as those set up in the laboratory, and it leads to extinction of both predator and prey.

There is a relatively easy way to circumvent the disastrous outcome of the unstable case, even without changing the positions of the two zero-growth curves. In this, the fourth case

(STABLE CYCLE WITH REFUGIUM), the prey is given a place to hide. As a result, there will always exist a certain number of prey organisms out of reach of the predator. Suppose that minnows were hunting oligochaete worms in a pond that offered secure hiding places for 1,000 worms. Then the minnows would crop down the worm population to this level and stop. Also, the minnow population would stop growing, or decline, until the worm population had a chance to increase again to the point of producing a surplus available to the minnows. The presence of a refugium is incorporated in the graph in Figure 10. Refugia occur commonly in nature and probably account for a great many of the balanced predator-prey systems that exist. It must be added that a refugium is not necessarily just a simple retreat which predators cannot penetrate. Instead it can be some remote area that the prey finds and colonizes before the predator is able to follow. The following example will illustrate this point. After several species of prickly pear cactus (*Opuntia*) were deliberately introduced into Australia from the New World, they grew so thickly that they became serious pests, rendering about 60 million acres impenetrable and unsuitable for grazing. The problem was solved when entomologists introduced the moth *Cactoblastis cactorum*, which feeds on the cactus in the caterpillar stage. The moth multiplied swiftly and consumed most of the *Opuntia* in Australia. But it did not eradicate the cactus entirely. There still exist small populations in isolated areas (the "refugia") which the moths are slow at finding. Thus the populations of the cactus and of its predator, the moth, are maintained in a stably oscillating state.

Finally, we should ask what biological justification exists for bending the zero-growth curves of the prey in the manner shown in Figures 9 and 10. It is not enough to say that this is an easy way to make the oscillations come out the way we wanted. These convex zero-growth curves are in fact more biologically realistic than the simpler Lotka-Volterra versions. To the left of the hump, as N_2 becomes small, the prey becomes scarce. The effect might be to make it more difficult for adults to find each other and to pair during the breeding season. Also, in species that feed socially, the flocks or schools might be smaller and hence less able to secure food. There exists, consequently, a value of N_2 below which the zero-growth curve will dip down. To the right, as N_2 becomes large, the prey individuals become more densely packed. Eventually density dependent factors besides predation itself will begin to increase mortality or decrease fertility in a disproportionate manner. The result will be a dip in the prey zero-growth curve to the right.

Volterra's principle. Volterra recognized the following surprising consequence of the Lotka-Volterra equations of the predator-prey system: If the two species are destroyed at the same rate by some outside agency, such as indiscriminate hunting or the use of pesticides by man, the prey will proportionately increase and the predators will proportionately decrease. In other words, if we destroy 50 percent of both the species, or any other percentage so long as it is about the same for both, the prey numbers will subsequently go up faster than those of the predator. This prediction follows from the equations, which we will repeat here:

$$\frac{dN_1}{dt} = B_1 N_1 N_2 - D_1 N_1 \qquad \text{Predator population growth}$$

$$\frac{dN_2}{dt} = B_2 N_2 - D_2 N_1 N_2 \qquad \text{Prey population growth}$$

Notice again that the product $N_1 N_2$ determines the birth rate of the predator and the death rate of the prey. If both N_1 and N_2 are reduced by the same proportionate amount, the effect will be much greater in the product $N_1 N_2$ than in N_1 or N_2 separately. Therefore the predator will have its birth rate more drastically cut, and the prey will have its death rate similarly reduced. The advantage will be to the prey. Consider a case in which there are originally 100 predators and 100 prey, so that $N_1 N_2 =$ 10,000. Now an outside agent destroys 50 percent of each of the two populations, so that N_1 and N_2 each contain 50 individuals. The new $N_1 N_2$ is not 50 percent of the old $N_1 N_2$; it is 2,500, or only 25 percent of the original quantity. No matter what the original values of N_1 and N_2, or the proportionate amount by which they are reduced, Volterra's principle will hold in theory. The principle may also have important implications in practice. Entomologists, for example, have noticed that when they attempt to control pest insect populations by spraying them with insecticides, the populations often spring back quickly to even higher levels than before. The effect has been traced to the simultaneous destruction of the natural predators and parasites of the pest species. In accordance with Volterra's principle, these beneficial insects are not able to recover as rapidly as the populations on which they feed.

FOOD WEBS AND POPULATION STABILITY

In the previous section on predation the populations of prey and predators were envisaged as discrete entities, changing in size as they interacted with each other. Now we will examine some of their properties as a system, enlarging the number of species involved in the interactions and considering the efficiency by which energy is exchanged from prey to predator. The act of consumption of members of a prey species by those of a predator species is called a LINK in a FOOD CHAIN. When more than one species in an ecosystem is consumed by a predator species, the set of links is called a FOOD WEB. Virtually all of the ecosystems of the world are comprised of very complex food webs, which can be broken down by analysis into interconnecting chains. The position located on the chain is referred to as the TROPHIC LEVEL. Thus the green plants, which capture radiant energy from the sun and are the producers for the community of species, comprise the first trophic level. The second trophic level is formed by the herbivores, which are the consumers of the green plants, the third trophic level by the carnivores, which eat the herbivores, the fourth trophic level by the secondary carnivores, which eat the carnivores, and so forth. In almost all ecosystems there are top carnivores, one or more large, specialized animal species that browse on the animals in the lower trophic levels but are not ordinarily consumed by predators themselves. The larger whales enjoy this status, and so do lions, wolves, and man himself, the most voracious of the top carnivores. In addition to the producer-to-carnivore chains (PREDATOR CHAINS) there are PARASITE CHAINS, in which small organisms feed on their larger hosts, usually without killing them outright, and DECOMPOSER CHAINS, in which bacteria, fungi, and a huge diversity of scavenger animal species feed on the dead tissues and products of organisms from all trophic levels.

It is part of the "conventional wisdom" of modern ecology that an increase in the number of links in the food web increases the STABILITY of the ecosystem. By this is meant that the more species of plants, herbivores, and carnivores that coexist, and the higher the number of links in which each species participates, the more each population will tend to vary around constant average levels and the more predictable will be the magnitude of the fluctuation. Also, the less the fluctuations are likely to become so extreme as to lead to extinction, and consequently the longer each species will persist in the ecosystem. The reasoning behind this inference is graphically represented in Figure 11. It can be succinctly put into words as follows. When a predator depends exclusively on a single prey species, there are many circumstances under which the two populations fluctuate widely— especially if they live in a simple environment. In the previous section you saw how the fluctuations can become unstable and result in the extinctions of the two populations. When there are

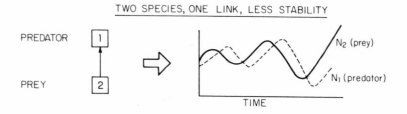

TWO SPECIES, ONE LINK, LESS STABILITY

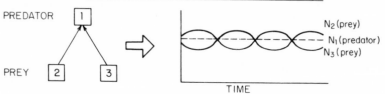

THREE SPECIES, TWO LINKS, MORE STABILITY

11 RELATIONSHIP BETWEEN SPECIES diversity and population stability. When a predator depends upon a single prey species, their populations can easily become unstable (*top*). But when two prey species are available, their independent fluctuations will tend to cancel out the fluctuations in the predator species (*bottom*).

two or more prey species, the chances for such catastrophic alterations are diminished. The reason is that when the first prey species is on the way down (hunted excessively, perhaps, by the predator), the second prey species may be on the way up (now consisting, perhaps, of life stages not pursued by the predator). The result is that the TOTAL number of prey belonging to both species will vary less than would be the case if only one prey species were available. The stabilizing effect depends on a SWITCHING RESPONSE on the part of the predator; that is, a tendency to hunt the more abundant prey in preference to the less abundant one. As one species builds up to excessive numbers, the predator exhibiting a switching response shifts its attention preferentially to this species, giving the less abundant prey species a better chance to multiply.

A great deal of evidence exists to suggest the general applicability of the diversity-stability rule, including the demonstration of the purely behavioral switching response in vertebrate and insect predators. The inference is used, for example, to account for the strong fluctuation often observed in arctic ecosystems and among the insect pests of agricultural monocultures (single-crop fields), both of which are characterized by low species diversity. However, the rule is not absolute. Recent evidence from studies of insect populations have shown that sometimes the existence of more than one predator species can result in wider fluctuations in the prey population. In other words, the opposite of the diversity-stability rule can occur. The reason is that some of the predator species can be unresponsive to changes in the prey population and yet still interfere enough with the responsive predators to allow the prey population to fluctuate widely. One responsive predator might have been able to damp the fluctuations if given a monopoly over the prey; but it is unable to do so when competing with other species. To what extent this reverse effect occurs in nature remains to be seen, but at least it serves to caution us—once again—that the simplest models of population ecology often fail in practice.

In Figure 12 are presented some food webs representing, in

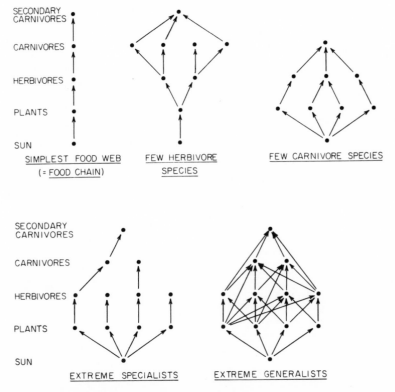

12   FOOD WEBS, consisting of interconnected food chains, in the species communities of different ecosystems.

oversimplified form, the entire communities of species in various ecosystems. These diagrams are intended to illustrate a couple of principles. First, the form of the food webs can vary drastically from one ecosystem to another. One ecosystem, for example red mangrove trees together with the animals living on them above the high tide line, can consist of a single plant species, a moderate number of herbivores, and a still larger number of carnivores. This is the situation represented in the middle diagram of the top row. Another ecosystem, such as a heavily grazed ranch, may contain a moderate diversity of plants and herbivores and only a single carnivore—in this case man. Most natural ecosystems, however, contain many species of plants, herbivores, and carnivores. The two diagrams in the lower row show how greatly ecosystems can differ from one another in the degree of food specialization. It is even possible, as indicated in the "extreme generalists" food web, for species to feed in more than one trophic level. Species that are both herbivores and carnivores, called OMNIVORES, are in fact abundant in most ecosystems.

PROBLEM. According to the diversity–stability rule, which of the five food webs diagrammed in Figure 12 should provide the greatest population stability for its member species?

ANSWER. The two food webs in the lower row should provide the greatest stability, because each contains a higher total species number (12) and, in most instances, a higher species number in each trophic level. Of the two arrays the "extreme generalists" should be more stable, because their web contains the greater number of food links.

PROBLEM. An ecosystem contains four species with all but the highest consumers providing food for all other species. Draw the two food webs which, according to the diversity-stability rule, provide the least stability and the greatest stability respectively.

ANSWER. The answer is provided in Figure 13. If we make three of the species plants and one a herbivore, only three links are possible. This should be the least stable community. At the other extreme, we can get six links out of four species if there is one plant species and three omnivorous species. According to theory, this would be the most stable community.

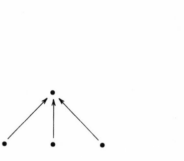

MINIMUM NUMBER OF LINKS (3)   MAXIMUM NUMBER
                                              OF LINKS (6)

13   TWO FOOD WEBS in a community of four species. On the left, the least stable community with only three links. On the right, the most stable community with six links.

THE MEASUREMENT OF DIVERSITY

When the diversity-stability rule was introduced in the last section, diversity was defined simply as the number of species. This is a valid measure for some kinds of investigations, but for most situations it is less than ideal. Often we need to know not only the number of species but also the relative abundance of each. Consider the matter of stability. If a predator depends on ten prey species that all have about the same abundance over long periods of time, we can expect each of the ten to play a comparable role in the regulation of the abundance of the predator. But now suppose that the system of ten prey species consists of a single very abundant species and nine very rare ones. The rare species might play a negligible role in the regulation of the predator population, which would then act as if it depends on a single species. Clearly some diversity measure is needed that incorporates information about the relative abundance of the species. Several such measures have been proposed. The one used most frequently is referred to variously as the ENTROPY MEASURE, the INFORMATION MEASURE, or the SHANNON-WIENER INFORMATION MEASURE

$$H_s = -\sum_{i=1}^{s} p_i \log p_i$$

H_S = the symbol for the amount of diversity in a group of S species; in this case the category of classification used is the species (hence the subscript S) but other categories could be used as well

S = the number of species in the group

p_i = the relative abundance of the ith species measured from 0 to 1.0 (for example, if the species under consideration is the second on the list, we label it $i = 2$; and if 10 per cent of all the individual organisms belong to that species, $p_i = 0.10$)

$\log p_i$ = the logarithm of p_i; it can be to the base 2, e, or 10; for convenience we will use the base e here, in other words the base of natural logarithms

The negative sign is added to make H come out positive. Otherwise the logarithms, which are all negative because p_i is between 0 and 1.0 when there are two or more i, would produce a negative sum. This diversity measure is popular among ecologists in part because it is the same as the entropy measure used in thermodynamics and the information measure used in information theory. In all three sciences—physics, communication mathematics, and ecology—H provides the degree of "uncertainty." A larger H means that if we are about to pick an atom, or a message, or an individual organism at random, we are less certain about which kind it is going to turn out to be. If there is only one species in an assemblage, for example, the uncertainty about the random organism is zero. Appropriately, the measure H will also be zero, because p of the species = 1, and the term $\log p = \log 1 = 0$. For any given number of species, H_S will be greatest if the species are all equally abundant. This, too, is intuitively satisfying, because the uncertainty about one particular organism is indeed highest if all of the possible species to which it can belong are equally likely.

The entropy measure of diversity has other advantages. First, it has no upper bound. That is, as species are added to the assemblage, H_S will tend to increase without limit; an infinite number of species, if that were conceivable, would produce an infinite H_S. Also, when different, independent classifications are applied to the same organisms, the separate entropy measures obtained from each can be simply added to provide the total amount of diversity for all. Suppose that in addition to counting up the organisms according to species, we decided to count them according to the food they eat (for example, 60 percent or 0.6

V. COMPUTATION OF THE ENTROPY MEASURE OF SPECIES

(See accompanying problem in text)

Species	p_i	$\log p_i$	$p_i \log p_i$
	First Group of Birds		
$i = 1$	0.2500	−1.3863	−0.346575
$i = 2$	0.2500	−1.3863	−0.346575
$i = 3$	0.2500	−1.3863	−0.346575
$i = 4$	0.2500	−1.3863	−0.346575
			−1.386300
			$H_s = 1.3863$

prey on birds, 0.2 prey on insects, etc.), or microhabitat (0.4 live in the tops of trees, 0.3 live at the bases of trees, etc.). Each new, independent classification yields its own H. Then one of the properties of the entropy measure is that all the H's can be summed to produce the total H. It is therefore possible to compare groups of organisms according to their diversity in a wide range of ecological traits. In most cases, however, the H you will encounter in the ecological literature is what we have labeled H_s, the diversity of species abundance.

PROBLEM. Two groups of bird species are sampled in the same forest. The first group consists of four equally abundant species. The second group consists of one species containing 50% of the individual birds, plus four other species that share the remaining individual birds equally. Which of the two groups of species has the greater diversity?

DIVERSITY (H_S) FOR TWO IMAGINARY GROUPINGS OF BIRD SPECIES

Species	p_i	$\log p_i$	$p_i \log p_i$
		Second Group of Birds	
$i = 1$	0.5000	−0.6932	−0.3466
$i = 2$	0.1250	−2.0794	−0.2599
$i = 3$	0.1250	−2.0794	−0.2599
$i = 4$	0.1250	−2.0794	−0.2599
$i = 5$	0.1250	−2.0794	−0.2599
			−1.3862
			$H_S = 1.3862$

ANSWER. The necessary computations are shown in Table V. The two groups turn out to have approximately the same H_S value and hence (by this definition) the same species diversity, despite their quite different abundance distributions.

PROBLEM. Which is the more diverse system: 2 equally abundant species, or 11 species, of which one contains 90 percent of the individuals and the remainder 1 percent each?

ANSWER. The two-species system, with $H_s = 0.6932$, is more diverse than the eleven-species system, with $H_s = 0.5553$.

ENERGY FLOW AND POPULATION TURNOVER

If you take the body of an animal and completely burn it in a microbomb calorimeter, so that all the energy it releases can be precisely measured, the animal will in most instances yield between 5 and 7 kilocalories for every gram of.its ash-free weight. In other words, for every gram of its body that can be burned up, the animal contains enough energy to heat somewhere between 5 and 7 kilograms of water by 1° C. Different kinds of animals vary little in this respect. Plants are much more variable, and they generally contain less energy. Predation and decomposition can be thought of as the capture of some of this energy by the feeding of organisms on the bodies of other organisms.

As energy flows through the various food chains, it is constantly divided into three channels. Some of it goes into PRODUCTION, which is the creation of new tissue by growth, development, and reproduction, together with the manufacture of energy-rich storage products in the form of fats and carbohydrates. Some of the energy is lost from the ecosystem by EXPORT, the emigration of organisms together with the passive transport of dead organic material out of the ecosystem by the actions of wind and water. The rest of the energy is lost permanently to the ecosystem and to all other ecosystems by means of RESPIRATION. The leakage due to respiration is very high. In fact, only a small fraction of the energy is transferred successfully from one trophic level to the next. Ecologists put the figure at roughly 10 percent. The exact measurement used to make this important generalization is ECOLOGICAL EFFICIENCY, which is defined as follows:

$$\text{Ecological efficiency} = \frac{\text{the calories produced by the population that are consumed by its predator}}{\text{the calories that the population consumes when feeding on its own prey}}$$

Suppose that we were studying the following very simple food chain: a field of clover, the mice that eat the clover, and the cats that eat the mice. According to the "ten percent rule" of ecological efficiency, we would expect that for every 100 calories of clover eaten by the mice per unit time, about 10 calories of mice would be eaten by the cats in the same unit of time. The ecological efficiency of the mice, with reference to the cats, is therefore ten percent:

$$\text{Ecological efficiency} = \frac{\text{the calories (10) of mice eaten by cats per unit time}}{\text{the calories (100) of clover eaten by mice per unit time}} \times 100\% = 10\%$$

Notice that the calories present in the clover are the same ones that the cats use. The cats, however, are specialized carnivores. They have sharp teeth that are adapted for seizing small animals and shearing meat. The mice, on the other hand, have teeth that are adapted for chopping and grinding seeds and other vegetable materials. Strictly from the point of view of the cat population, the mouse population is a device for converting clover calories into a useable form. Our generalization states that the best mice can do is to make available ten percent of the clover calories they eat to the cats. If something else ate cats they would find these animals about equally efficient at converting mouse calories. Measurements in diverse ecosystems and laboratory experiments have shown that the ecological efficiencies actually vary from about 5 to 20 percent. Most are close enough to 10 percent to make this figure useful for rough first approximations only.

Ecological efficiencies can be calculated for entire trophic levels as well as for single populations. For example, a study by H. T. Odum of the aquatic ecosystem at Silver Springs, Florida, yielded the following measurements of kilocalories captured, stored, and passed on to the next trophic level under each square meter of water surface per year.

Plants		Herbivores		Carnivores		Secondary carnivores	
Entering	Stored	Entering	Stored	Entering	Stored	Entering	Stored
20,810	8,833	3,368	1,478	383	67	21	6

The ecological efficiencies of the first three levels are: the plants $3,368/20,810 = 16$ percent; the herbivores $383/3,368 = 11$ percent; the carnivores $21/383 = 5.5$ percent.

In addition to the variability in ecological efficiency that exists from level to level and from species to species, a second complicating factor in the analysis of energy flow is the fact that species cannot always be neatly sorted into trophic levels. Individual species, particularly the omnivores, sometimes play multiple roles. The crow, for example, is both a predator of insects and other small animals and a scavenger of dead birds and mammals—and therefore a decomposer. Some other birds feed on fruits and seeds, which makes them herbivores, and also on a wide variety of insects, which makes them first and second level carnivores. Yet even with these qualifications, the ten-percent rule of ecological efficiency can be used to account for an important general feature of the organization of ecosystems: Food chains seldom have more than four or five links.

The reason is that a 90 percent reduction (approximately) in productivity results in only $1/10 \times 1/10 \times 1/10 \times 1/10 = 1/10,000$ of the energy removed from the green plants being available to the fifth trophic level. In fact, the top carnivore that is utilizing only one-ten-thousandth as many calories as produced by the plants on which it ultimately depends must be both sparsely distributed and far-ranging in its activities. Wolves feeding on moose must travel as much as 20 miles a day to find enough energy. The ranges of tigers and other big cats often cover hundreds of square miles. And such organisms are simply too sparse to support predators on their own. No animal species preys on tigers—probably less because tigers are formidable than because they produce too few calories to make the effort worthwhile.

PROBLEM. Suppose that there are eight species of animals in an ecosystem: A, B, C, D, E, F, G, and H. Species A preys on species B and C, species B preys on species D, species C preys on species E, species D preys on species F and H, species E preys on species F and G. Draw the food web for this community. How many trophic levels are there and which species are on each? If 1,000 units of energy are transferred from the lowest trophic level to the next trophic level in a day, roughly how many units of energy would you expect to be received at the highest trophic level?

ANSWER. The food web is shown in Figure 14. There are four trophic levels. The energy (1,000 units/day) is received by the second level from the bottom. We are interested in how much of it reaches two levels beyond. If we guess according to the ten percent rule, the amount would be $1/10 \times 1/10 \times 1000 = 10$ units/day. Recalling that known ecological efficiencies vary by as much as 5 percent to 20 percent, the most conservative reasonable guess would be $1/20 \times 1/20 \times 1000 = 2.5$ units/day; and the most generous reasonable guess would be $1/5 \times 1/5 \times 1000 = 40$ units/day.

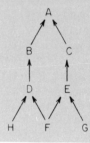

14   FOOD WEB for eight species of animals (four trophic levels).

Beginning students of marine ecology make a puzzling discovery when they examine their first plankton sample: The floating organisms of the sea consist mostly of copepod crustaceans and other invertebrate animals; these little predators outweigh the algal cells on which they feed by as much as two to one. How can such a top-heavy system be maintained? After all, we just noted that herbivores harvest only about 10 percent of the energy captured by the plants on which they feed. The answer is that the algal cells produce calories much faster than do the planktonic animals. They metabolize and grow more quickly and consequently they are able to reproduce at least as fast as they are being destroyed by the herbivores. It is a general rule of physiology that the smaller the individual organism, the higher its metabolic and growth rates. Among species of algae, for example, a 25-fold decrease in size (measured by the surface-to-volume ratio) results in a 5-fold increase in productivity. Since the planktonic algae are among the world's smallest plants, it is less surprising that lower numbers can support a relatively large mass of herbivores.

It is generally true that only a loose relationship exists between the amount of living material at each level of the ecosystem, usually referred to as its BIOMASS or STANDING CROP,

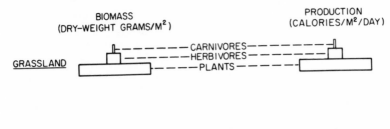

15 BIOMASS PYRAMIDS and energy pyramids in two different
ecosystems. The biomass pyramid shows the total weight of organisms belonging to the different trophic levels that are encountered
in a circumscribed area at any given instant of time. The energy
pyramid shows the rate of production in the different levels.

and its rate of production. Figure 15 presents examples of the
diagrams often used by ecologists to express these two properties
of whole communities of organisms. The BIOMASS PYRAMID
shows the total weight of organisms belonging to the different
trophic levels that are encountered in a circumscribed area, in
this case one square meter, at any given instant of time. The
ENERGY PYRAMID shows the rate of production, in calories per
unit time, in the different levels. As you might expect from the
ten percent rule of ecological efficiency, energy pyramids are
very similar from one ecosystem to the next. However, because
of the extreme variation in size and productivity of different
kinds of organisms, for example algae versus redwood trees,
the biomass pyramids vary greatly.

The relation between biomass and energy can be made more
explicit by utilizing the concept of TURNOVER, defined as the
replacement of organisms that have been removed. Turnover
occurs in both individual organisms that are eaten and in the
calories they contain. It is related to the biomass of the prey
population and to the average life span of prey organisms in the
following way. Suppose that the population of cats we were
just discussing required a diet of 10,000 kilocalories of mice a
day. If each mouse weighs 20 grams, and each gram yields 5
kilocalories, then each mouse contains 5×20 kilocalories =
100 kilocalories. The cats therefore must catch

$$\frac{10,000 \text{ kilocalories/day}}{100 \text{ kilocalories/mouse}} = 100 \text{ mice/day}$$

One hundred mice per day (or 10,000 kilocalories of mice per day) is the turnover rate in the mouse population. How large a biomass is required to yield such a turnover rate? It depends on the life span of the average mouse. Suppose that each mouse lives an average of 50 days, and then is caught by a cat. This means that each day the cats eliminate 1/50 of the mouse population. Therefore the total mouse population is

$$50 \times \text{(turnover rate in mice)}$$
$$= 50 \times 100 \text{ mice}$$
$$= 5,000 \text{ mice}$$

The longer the average life span of the prey organism, the larger the prey population must be in order to support a given population of predators. The relationship, as you can see, is a simple reciprocal one.

PROBLEM. In pond A a population of crustaceans is supported by a standing crop of approximately ten billion algal cells. The average cell lives for two days before being consumed. In pond B a similar population of the same species of crustacean lives on a second species of alga, identical to the first in physiology and ecology except that the average cell lives an average of only one day. Predict the standing crop of algal cells in pond B.

ANSWER. Five billion cells are the expected standing crop of the alga in pond B. Note that pond A and pond B yield the same number of cells to their respective crustacean consumers each day. However, the algal population in A does it by giving up the equivalent of its whole population every two days, that is, 10 billion/2 days = 5 billion/day. The algal population in B does the same thing by giving up the equivalent of its entire population each day. Since its rate of turnover is the same as in A, 5 billion/day, its standing crop must be 5 billion cells.

PROBLEM. A population of sowbugs living in a field supports a population of spiders. One year the grass grows longer, with the result that the sowbugs become harder to catch and their average life span is doubled. Despite this change in life history, their number remains the same. If everything else remains equal, what will be the effect of the longer grass on the spider population?

ANSWER. The number of spiders in the population will decrease. If the great majority of the sowbugs are adults, which would be the case if most of their life were spent as adults, the population of spiders would be cut approximately in half by the doubling of the sowbug life span.

However, if much of the sowbug life span is spent in small immature stages, the decrease in the spider population would not be as great. Can you see why?

COMPETITION

Competition is defined by ecologists as the active demand by two or more organisms for a common vital resource. When the resource is not sufficient to meet the requirements of all of the organisms seeking it, it becomes a limiting factor in population growth. When, in addition, the shortage of the resource limits growth with increasing severity as the organisms become more numerous, then competition is by definition one of the density dependent factors. The techniques of competition are extremely diverse. An animal that aggressively challenges another over a piece of food is obviously competing. So is another animal that marks its territory with a scent, even when other animals avoid the territory solely because of the odor and without ever seeing the territorial owner. Competition also includes the using up of resources to the detriment of other organisms, whether or not any aggressive behavioral interaction occurs. A plant, for example, may absorb phosphates through its root system at the expense of its neighbors, or cut off its neighbors from sunlight by shading them with its leaves.

Competition can occur among members of the same species (INTRASPECIFIC COMPETITION) or between individuals belonging to different species (INTERSPECIFIC COMPETITION). Ecologists have focused most of their theory and observation on interspecific competition, and that is the subject we will explore here. The central issue of such competition theory is the elucidation of the conditions under which competing species either mutually exclude each other as a result of competition, or else achieve an accommodation that allows them to coexist for indefinite periods of time. Both events have been commonly documented in nature. Like predation theory, competition theory is concerned with the regulation of population growth. In fact, as you will see shortly, the elementary equations of competition contain several of the same parameters used in describing the effects of predation. It is traditional in presenting the theory of this subject to start with the equations, proceed to the graphical analysis based on the equations, and finally—if ever—to relate the theory intuitively to observations of competition in nature. In the treatment that follows we will reverse the sequence, in the belief that this permits the most effective possible introduction to a beginning student.

Recognition of the fact of competition between two species raises the obvious question: Why don't the two encroach on each another until one becomes extinct? The answer is that if a pair of species are too similar to one another in their requirements, one of them does indeed go extinct. This generalization is usually referred to as GAUSE'S PRINCIPLE (after G. F. Gause, one of the pioneer investigators of competition), or else as the PRINCIPLE OF COMPETITIVE EXCLUSION. It can be stated in broad terms as follows: NO TWO SPECIES THAT ARE ECOLOGI-CALLY IDENTICAL CAN LONG COEXIST. The idea of ecological identity versus ecological difference can be more easily grasped by considering the concept of the NICHE. Each species, or more precisely each local population, has a temperature range in which it can successfully live and reproduce itself. It also has an array of foods on which it can subsist. In the case of plants, each population has a certain set of nutrients it must absorb from the soil, in addition to the basic requirement of solar energy. Furthermore, there exists a particular range of humidity within which the population can grow. So far we have listed three "dimensions" of the niche—temperature, nutrients, and humidity. The list can be greatly lengthened. One might add, for example, the times of the day and the seasons of the year in which the species is active, the major habitat in which it lives, and so on. In this straightforward manner the niche of the population can be analyzed, component by component, until a fairly complete picture of the ecological requirements of the population is developed.

The principle of competitive exclusion, then, states that unless the niches of two species differ, the species cannot coexist. The implication is that if the two species are so genetically similar that their niches are the same, they cannot occupy the same geographical range. It is also true that the two species can be genetically different but find themselves in a particular environment where they are forced to live in the same place and do the same things. In this case also, one species will replace the other. The pair of species can coexist only if new pieces of the environment are added in such a way that one part favors one species and the other part favors the second species. For example, when two species of flour beetles, belonging to the genera *Tribolium* and *Oryzaephilus*, are required to live and breed in a simple receptacle containing nothing but flour, *Tribolium* always extinguishes *Oryzaephilus*. But when this environment is complicated by the addition of fine-glass tubing to the flour, the two species can coexist. The reason is that the tubing allows the *Oryzaephilus* to hold its own in part of the environment even though it loses out in the remainder. Its niche, in other words, is sufficiently different from that of *Tribolium* to permit it to coexist in some environments.

The concept of the niche alone permits only a crude understanding of competitive exclusion. There is much more to the story than just the tolerance limits of the competing species. In order to gain a fuller picture we need to return to the basic theory of population growth, and in particular to consider the growth rates of the two species. COMPETITIVE EXCLUSION OCCURS IF ONE SPECIES PRODUCES ENOUGH INDIVIDUALS TO PREVENT THE POPULATION OF THE OTHER FROM INCREASING. This will not happen if the niches of the two species are different enough so that each species enjoys a portion of the environment where it cannot be suppressed by excessive numbers of its competitors. Each species will tend to increase logistically, that is, until it has reached its own equilibrium population size (by definition, $N = K$). If, at this point, its numbers are not so great as to reverse population growth in the other species, and the second species reciprocates, coexistence is possible. In Figure 16 we have presented an imaginary example involving two species of moths to illustrate the relationship between logistic growth, specialization into different niches, and competitive exclusion. Here the dimension of the niche that has been diversified is the place where the moths live and breed. We could have just as easily made it the time in which they live and breed, or the part of the forest that they favor, or any of a number of other ecological properties, singly or in combination.

Next consider the graphical models proposed in Figures 17 and 18. Note (in Figure 17) the basic postulate that there exists a set of joint values of N_1 (horizontal axis) and N_2 (vertical axis) along which N_1, the number of organisms in species 1, is neither increasing nor decreasing. This set of joint values falls along the straight line labeled $dN_1/dt = 0$. A similar set of joint values also exists in which N_2, the number of organisms in species 2, is stationary; these values fall along the line labeled $dN_2/dt = 0$. Outside its zero-growth line the species indicated is decreasing, because there are too many organisms for the environment to support. Inside the line its numbers are increasing, because the environment has not yet been filled up. Why are the values of N_1 and N_2 considered jointly in this way? Implied in the two lines is the negative effect of competition. An increase in N_1 means that something is being taken away from species 2 that diminishes its growth rate; and an increase in N_2 likewise decreases the growth rate of species 1. The presence of one species means also that the other species

16   BASIC CONDITIONS for the coexistence of two species. The equilibrium population of the black moth species, which is specialized for life in the oak tree (*left*), is too small to send enough individuals to the fir tree to eliminate the white moth species (*right*). The same equilibrium condition exists for the white moth species on the fir tree.

will stop increasing at a lower abundance. This is why the zero-growth lines pass from one axis to the other axis in the manner suggested. You can see, for example, that the higher the value of N_1, the lower the value of N_2 at which species 2 stops growing, in other words the value of N_2 at which $dN_2/dt = 0$.

Now consider population growth in the two species simultaneously. In Case 1, the zero-growth line for species 1 lies outside that for species 2. This means that for joint abundances between the two lines, species 1 is increasing while species 2 is decreasing. The joint abundances will change with time in the direction indicated by the arrows: N_1 positive, N_2 negative, until finally the joint abundance reaches the equilibrium point —at which $N_2 = 0$. Thus species 2 is inexorably eliminated in the competition. The same result is obtained regardless of the

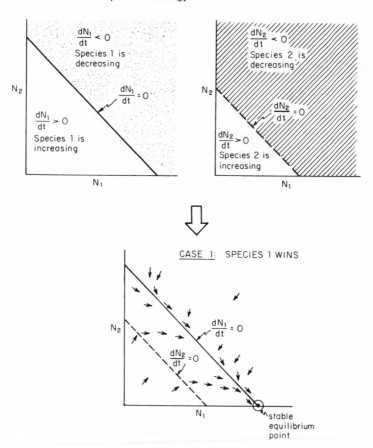

17 COMPETITION BETWEEN TWO SPECIES. The zero-growth curve for species 1, labeled $dN_1/dt = 0$, falls outside the zero-growth curve for species 2, labeled $dN_2/dt = 0$. As a consequence, changes in joint abundance through time, indicated by the arrows, always favor species 1 at the expense of species 2 and lead ultimately to the extinction of species 2.

starting position for the joint abundances of the two species, whether inside both zero-growth curves, or outside both, or in between them.

The four possible outcomes of competition are best understood by studying the graphs in Figures 17 and 18 and marking arrows of your own to plot the joint abundances. The outcome with the greatest interest is the one marked Case 4, which presents the conditions required for stable coexistence.

How can these abstractions be related to the intuitive explanation given earlier for stable coexistence? Recall that it was said that for two species to live together indefinitely, they must stop increasing before they produce enough individuals to reverse the growth of the competing species. Their own density dependent controls bring their growth to a halt before they eliminate the competitor. This is what is implied in the graph of Case 4. As species 1 increases and species 2 decreases, the two must eventually reach a point where this process is reversed. Species 1 is then so abundant that its own density dependent controls halt its growth, but—because its niche is

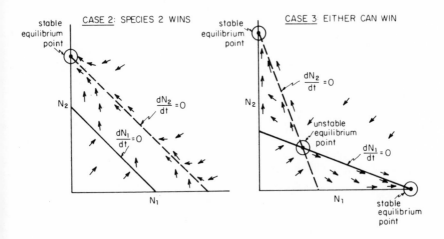

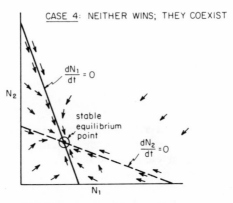

18   COMPETITION BETWEEN TWO SPECIES. The remaining three, of four, possible outcomes.

sufficiently different—not so abundant that it can stop species 2 from beginning to increase. The symmetrical relationship occurs with respect to species 2. Eventually the joint abundance reaches the stable equilibrium point, where (theoretically!) no further change occurs through time.

In order to complete the analysis, we must state the theory in terms of growth equations. Why, in particular, were the zero-growth curves drawn as straight lines with negative slopes? The reason is the form of the basic competition equations, which incorporate the simplest possible assumptions about the interference between two species. When one of the species, say species 1, occurs by itself, its growth can be expected to proceed at least roughly in accordance with the logistic equation:

$$\frac{dN_1}{dt} = r_1 N_1 \left(\frac{K_1 - N_1}{K_1} \right)$$

where each term is given the subscript 1 to indicate that its value is peculiar to species 1. When N_1 reaches K_1, $dN_1/dt = 0$; in other words, growth stops. Now let us add species 2 to the system. Its presence reduces the capacity of the environment for species 1. Clearly, this capacity (K_1) must be reduced by that amount of the environment used by species 2, which in turn is proportional to the number of individuals in species 2. In the simplest model this quantity is αN_2, where α is a constant. The logistic equation for species 1 can now be modified to incorporate the effect of the competitor:

$$\frac{dN_1}{dt} = r_1 N_1 \left(\frac{(K_1 - \alpha N_2) - N_1}{K_1} \right)$$
$$= r_1 N_1 \left(\frac{K_1 - N_1 - \alpha N_2}{K_1} \right)$$

Symmetrically, species 2 will be affected by species 1 as follows:

$$\frac{dN_2}{dt} = r_2 N_2 \left(\frac{(K_2 - \beta N_1) - N_2}{K_2} \right)$$
$$= r_2 N_2 \left(\frac{K_2 - N_2 - \beta N_1}{K_2} \right)$$

What these COMPETITION EQUATIONS say is simply that the presence of one species reduces the amount of environment (indicated by K) available to the other. The constant α is referred to as the COMPETITION COEFFICIENT of species 2 with respect to species 1, while β is the reverse competition coefficient. Suppose that species 1 and 2 were small crustaceans competing for a limiting production of algal cells, and that one individual of species 2 ate 2 cells for every one eaten by an individual of species 1. Then as far as the carrying capacity of the environment for species 1 is concerned, the presence of one individual of species 2 is the equivalent of the presence of 2 individuals of its own species. In other words, $\alpha = 2$.

By setting the two competition equations each equal to zero, we obtain the two zero-growth curves used in the graphical analysis presented earlier:

$$\frac{dN_1}{dt} = r_1 N_1 \left(\frac{K_1 - N_1 - \alpha N_2}{K_1}\right) = 0 \qquad \text{Species 1}$$

$$N_1 = K_1 - \alpha N_2 \qquad \text{zero-growth curve for species 1}$$

$$\frac{dN_2}{dt} = r_2 N_2 \left(\frac{K_2 - N_2 - \beta N_2}{K_2}\right) = 0 \qquad \text{Species 2}$$

$$N_2 = K_2 - \beta N_1 \qquad \text{zero-growth curve for species 2}$$

Next, setting N_1 and then N_2 equal to zero in each of the two zero-growth curves, we obtain the values of the intercepts (see Figure 19).

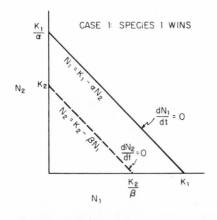

19 ZERO-GROWTH CURVES for two species in competition (Case 1).

PROBLEM. Two species are in competition in the form described by the elementary competition equations. For some time the population size of species 1 has been near 100 individuals and that of its competitor, species 2, has been near 700 individuals. The competition coefficient is the same for both species and is equal to 0.7. What population sizes could each species attain if its competitor were absent?

ANSWER. To solve the problem it is necessary to obtain the values of K_1 and K_2. The populations are evidently in a state of equilibrium ($N_1 = 100$; $N_2 = 700$), so that the equations for the zero-growth curves can be used. For the first species this is

$$N_1 = K_1 - \alpha N_2$$
$$100 = K_1 - 0.7 \times 700$$
$$K_1 = 590$$

For the second species, the same procedure is followed:

$$N_2 = K_2 - \beta N_1$$
$$700 = K_2 - 0.7 \times 100$$
$$K_2 = 770$$

Suggested Additional Reading

Connell, J. H., D. B. Mertz, and W. W. Murdoch, eds. 1970. READINGS IN ECOLOGY AND ECOLOGICAL GENETICS. Harper & Row, Publishers, Incorporated, New York. *viii* + 397 pp. (An excellent collection of research articles, overlapping in subject matter with Hazen's collection cited below, but with a stronger emphasis on evolutionary aspects. The *Primer* should be enough to permit you to proceed directly to these original research materials.)

Dawson, P. S., and C. E. King, eds. 1971. READINGS IN POPULATION BIOLOGY. Prentice-Hall, Inc., Englewood Cliffs, New Jersey. (A very useful collection of research articles in both population genetics and ecology, for which the *Primer* serves as an adequate theoretical introduction.)

Hazen, W. E., ed. 1970. READINGS IN POPULATION AND COMMUNITY ECOLOGY. 2d ed. W. B. Saunders Company, Philadelphia. *ix* + 421 pp. (A collection of research articles similar to that edited by Connell *et al.* but more strictly limited to the traditional topics of ecology.)

Medawar, P. B. 1957. THE UNIQUENESS OF THE INDIVIDUAL. Methuen & Co., Ltd., London. 191 pp. (This book contains Medawar's original essay on the evolution of senescence, for students who wish to pursue the subject further. It is seldom discussed in textbooks on evolution and population biology. Another key reference is the article by W. D. Hamilton, "The Moulding of Senescence," in the *Journal of Theoretical Biology* 12:12–45; 1966.)

Odum, E. P. 1971. FUNDAMENTALS OF ECOLOGY. 3d ed. W. B. Saunders Company, Philadelphia. *xvi* + 688 pp. (Perhaps the best general textbook, but one that is much stronger on empirical materials than on theory.)

Pielou, E. C. 1969. AN INTRODUCTION TO MATHEMATICAL ECOLOGY. Interscience Publishers, New York. *viii* + 286 pp. (A lucid and thorough mathematical treatment of some of the basic ideas of population and community ecology. This book can serve as the mathematician's introduction to advanced ecology, but it is also strongly recommended to biology students as the next step in mathematical model building after they leave the *Primer*.)

Slobodkin, L. B. 1962. GROWTH AND REGULATION OF ANIMAL POPULATIONS. Holt, Rinehart, and Winston Inc., New York. *viii* + 184 pp. (A clear, provocative, and often profound essay on most of the central topics of population ecology.)

Southwood, T. R. E. 1966. ECOLOGICAL METHODS WITH PARTICULAR REFERENCE TO THE STUDY OF INSECT POPULATIONS. Methuen & Co., Ltd., London. *xviii* + 391 pp. (This valuable book shows the connections that can be made between basic theory and many kinds of experimental and field studies, and it describes the practical methods for conducting empirical research.)

Watt, K. E. F. 1968. ECOLOGY AND RESOURCE MANAGEMENT. McGraw-Hill Book Company, Inc., New York. *xii* + 450 pp. (This book is highly recommended reading for students who wish to go forward in ecology and population biology. The author expounds the necessity of developing "complex theory," involving systems of equations far more complex and specific than those offered in the *Primer*, in order to solve practical problems in ecology. His viewpoint is different from that of Pielou, who stresses models and equations that are less precise but more general in application. The two books should by all means be read in conjunction.)

Whittaker, R. H. 1970. COMMUNITIES AND ECOSYSTEMS. The Macmillan Company, New York. *xi* + 162 pp. (A contemporary review of some of the principal topics of community ecology, with a strong emphasis on field analysis.)

Woodwell, G. M. and H. H. Smith, eds. 1969. DIVERSITY AND STABILITY IN ECOLOGICAL SYSTEMS. Brookhaven Symposia in Biology, No. 22. 264 pp. (A collection of research and review articles which presents the modern view of these most complex subjects of ecology.)

4 Biogeography: Species Equilibrium Theory

The living world is broken into patches. It exists to a large extent either on "real" islands, such as bodies of land projecting from the sea, or "habitat islands," which are fragments of habitats surrounded by other habitats of markedly different nature. Figure 1 provides an intuitive aid to this view of nature. Notice that whereas only a geographic unit of the magnitude of Bermuda or Cuba is an island to a bird, a single spruce tree in the middle of a field can be an island to an insect, and a teaspoon of water serves as one to a microorganism. The islands contain sets of species that can be demarcated as more or less discrete communities. In analyzing such units, ecologists and biogeographers wish to learn the principles and laws that govern the buildup of species during the colonization period, the final equilibrium level attained, and the immigration and extinction rates of species throughout the process. The section to follow will familiarize you with the basic theory of this subject, which has only recently been put into mathematical form and is now in the process of being tested and extended.

THE AREA-SPECIES CURVE

Very roughly, the number of species belonging to a given taxon increases as approximately the cube root to the fourth root of the area of the island. An example can be taken from the reptile-and-amphibian faunas of the West Indies (Figure 2). Here $S = CA^{0.301}$, where S is the number of species, A is the area of the island, and C is the value of S at $A = 1$ (its value is not important for our purposes). Notice that the scale used in the graph is doubly logarithmic, giving a straight-line area-

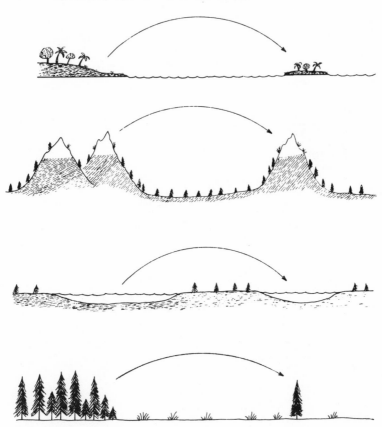

1   "TRUE ISLANDS" (*top*) and "habitat islands" (*bottom three*) are analyzed by the same quantitative theory.

species curve; and since $\log S = \log C + 0.301 \log A$, the slope of this curve is 0.301.

PROBLEM. Suppose you are an entomologist exploring the ant fauna of southeastern Asia. You have just completed a thorough study of a small island (area: 100 square miles) and found it to hold 10 ant species. Previous studies have shown that the slopes of ant area-species curves in a log-log plot are about 0.30. Now you are about to explore a much larger island (area: 10,000 square miles). Predict the number of ant species on this larger, unstudied island.

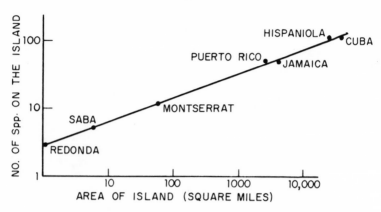

2   AREA-SPECIES CURVE of reptiles and amphibians in the West Indies.

ANSWER. From the information just given we predict that for most cases $S = CA^{0.30}$. We know from our explored island that $10 = C \times 100^{0.30}$. We could determine C at this point and then solve for 10,000, but it is better to take a short cut by simply dividing the two equations, canceling out C and solving directly for the unknown S, as follows:

$$\frac{S}{10} = \frac{C \times 10{,}000^{0.30}}{C \times 100^{0.30}}$$

$$S = 40 \text{ ant species}$$

THE EQUILIBRIUM MODEL

The regularity of the area-species relation and certain corre-lations observed between the slope of the area-species curve and the degree of isolation of the islands prompted MacArthur and Wilson (1967) to construct the following basic equilibrium model. First, note that as an island fills up with species, the total IMMIGRATION RATE (λ_S), defined as the number of new species arriving per unit time, should drop, as in Figure 3.

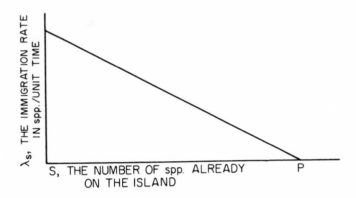

3   IMMIGRATION CURVE. As species fill the island, the rate of arrival of new species drops.

P represents the number of species in the "pool," that is, the number found in the surrounding source areas. Note that if, by some unlikely circumstance, there already exist P species on our island, the immigration rate is zero by definition.

Now, similarly, we should expect the TOTAL EXTINCTION RATE (μ_S), defined as the rate at which species *already on the island* go extinct, to rise as shown in Figure 4. In order to simplify matters, we are employing here the linear model, where the rate curves are given as straight. A great many reasonable modi-fications in the shape of the rate curves could be postulated, without, however, altering the qualitative conclusions drawn by the linear model.

When $\lambda_S = \mu_S$, the number of species will be at equilibrium, a species number designated by S (see Figure 5).

Now, what is the total immigration rate (λ_S) in number of species per unit time when S species are present? First, take the average immigration rate of new species, per species, onto the island when S species are present; let us label it λ_A. The

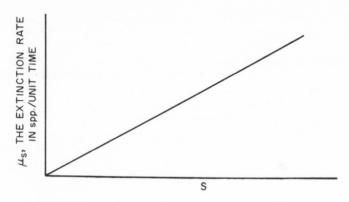

4 EXTINCTION CURVE. As species fill up the island, the rate at which they become extinct increases.

total immigration rate is this number λ_A (which is a constant in the linear equilibrium model) times the number not yet on the island, or λ_A $(P - S)$. Next, what is the total extinction rate in species per unit time? It is the average extinction rate per species μ_A, also a constant in our simple model, times the number of species already on the island, or $\mu_A S$. Finally, what is the rate of increase with time (dS/dt) in the number of

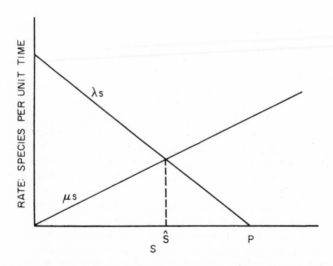

5 BASIC MODEL of species equilibrium. At $\hat{S}$, enough species are present so that the extinction rate equals the immigration rate.

species on the island? It is the total immigration rate minus the total extinction rate:

$$\frac{dS}{dt} = \lambda_S - \mu_S \qquad [1]$$
$$= \lambda_A(P - S) - \mu_A S$$

At equilibrium, $dS/dt = 0$ by definition, so that

$$\frac{dS}{dt}\bigg|_{S = \hat{S}} = \lambda_A(P - \hat{S}) - \mu_A\hat{S} = 0$$

(Note that at equilibrium the number of species is labeled $\hat{S}$.) By rearrangement,

$$\hat{S} = \frac{\lambda_A P}{\lambda_A + \mu_A} \qquad [2]$$

PROBLEM. A small offshore island was defaunated near a larger, source island containing 210 species of arthropods. After a short period of time the small island was found to contain 10 arthropod species, the total immigration rate was estimated to be one species every 5 days and the total extinction rate was estimated to be one species every 10 days. Predict the equilibrium number of species from the linear model.

ANSWER. The linear model predicts that $\hat{S} = \lambda_A P/(\lambda_A + \mu_A)$. P is given as 210 species. λ_A (the average immigration rate) is the total immigration rate divided by the number of species not yet on the island, or $(1/5)/(210 - 10) = 0.001$. μ_A (the average extinction rate) is the total extinction rate divided by the number of species already on the island, or $(1/10)/10 = 0.01$. Inserting these numbers in the equation, we get $\hat{S} \doteq 19$ species.

We have just shown how the linear equilibrium model can be used in an attempt to predict the ultimate equilibrium species number from a knowledge of the immigration and extinction rates. Let us now turn the prediction process around. We reasoned that

$$\frac{dS}{dt} = \lambda_A(P - S) - \mu_A S$$

If you have had enough calculus, try to confirm the following solution of this differential equation (if you haven't, inspect the result closely just the same):

$$S = \frac{\lambda_A P}{\lambda_A + \mu_A}\,(1 - e^{-(\lambda_A + \mu_A)t}) \qquad [3]$$

As t becomes very large, $e^{-(\lambda_A + \mu_A)t}$ approaches zero, and S approaches $\hat{S}$ $[= \lambda_A P/(\lambda_A + \mu_A)]$, as we observed already in Equation 2. We use the rate of approach to equilibrium to derive the TURNOVER EQUATION that predicts the rate of turnover ($=$ extinction rate $=$ immigration rate) at equilibrium. We first select some arbitrary fraction of $\hat{S}$, say 90 percent of $\hat{S}$, or $0.9\hat{S}$. Now multiply both sides of Equation 2 by 0.9 to obtain

$$0.9\hat{S} = \frac{\lambda_A P}{\lambda_A + \mu_A} \times 0.9 \qquad [4]$$

Bear in mind that $S = 0.9\hat{S}$ by our arbitrary selection; next we apply Equation 3 and note that

$$S = 0.9\hat{S} = \frac{\lambda_A P}{\lambda_A + \mu_A}\,(1 - e^{-(\lambda_A + \mu_A)t_{0.9}}) \qquad [5]$$

Compare Equations 4 and 5 to see that

$$1 - e^{-(\lambda_A + \mu_A)t_{0.9}} = 0.9$$

where $t_{0.9}$ is the time required for the island to fill up to 90 percent of its equilibrium number. By rearranging and taking natural logarithms (you should try this yourself for practice) we get

$$t_{0.9} = \frac{2.3}{\lambda_A + \mu_A} \qquad [6]$$

where (don't forget!) λ_A and μ_A are the *average* immigration and extinction rates respectively. We could stop here and put this equation to immediate use, but let's first get it into a more useful form by converting to the total rates λ_S and μ_S. MacArthur and Wilson (1967:38), for purposes of illustration, took the simplifying step of letting $\lambda_A = \mu_A$, so that

$$t_{0.9} = \frac{2.3}{2\mu_A} = \frac{1.2}{\mu_A}$$

If you now multiply the right-hand side of the equation by $\hat{S}/\hat{S} = 1$, you get (for this special case)

$$t_{0.9} = \frac{1.2\hat{S}}{\mu_{\hat{S}}} \qquad [7]$$

where $\mu_{\hat{S}}$ is the total extinction rate at equilibrium.

PROBLEM. A series of small, undisturbed islands have about 30 plant species each; floristic surveys over a period of several years have indicated that average immigration rates are about equal to average extinction rates; and the total extinction rate is shown to be one species per year per island. A severe hurricane one September day completely destroys the vegetation of one of the islands. About how long will it take for the flora to return to, say, 90 percent of its original number?

ANSWER.

$$t_{0.9} = \frac{1.2 \times 30 \text{ species}}{1 \text{ species/year}} = 36 \text{ years}$$

PROBLEM. Here is a real example. The island of Krakatau (or Krakatoa), located in the Sunda Strait between Sumatra and Java, suffered a huge volcanic eruption in 1883 that destroyed its entire fauna. Birds later recolonized the island (along with almost all other important elements of the fauna and flora), reaching an apparent equilibrium of approximately 27 species in a period of 36 years. Using the elementary equilibrium model, predict the turnover rate at equilibrium.

ANSWER.

$$\mu_{\hat{s}} = \frac{1.2 \times 27}{36} = 0.9 \text{ species/year}$$

From the data of K. W. Dammerman, MacArthur and Wilson obtained an estimated minimal turnover rate of 0.4 species/year. Similar approximations, correct to the nearest order of magnitude, have since been obtained from the elementary model applied to colonization data of fresh-water benthic organisms and island-dwelling insects and other arthropods.

PROBLEM. Let us now try for a little more flexibility by making λ_A *not* equal to μ_A. Suppose the little islands had their 30 species drawn from a nearby mainland containing 130 species. Again, we measure a total immigration rate for each island of one new species per year. Before going on, what are λ_A and μ_A?

ANSWER. λ_A by definition is the average immigration rate, equal to the total immigration rate (1 species per year) divided by the number of species in the pool *not* on the island ($P - \hat{S} = 130 - 30 = 100$). So $\lambda_A = 1/100$. What is μ_A? We know that since the islands are at equilibrium, the total extinction rate is equal to the total immigration rate, or 1 species per year. μ_A by definition is this total extinction rate divided by the number of species already on the island, or $1/30$.

PROBLEM. One of the islands is completely denuded by a storm. How long will it take this island to regain 90 percent of the original species number?

ANSWER. From Equation 6, $t_{0.9} = 2.3/(1/100 + 1/30) = $ 53 years. Notice that to solve this problem, in which we did not take it for granted that $\lambda_A = \mu_A$, we needed to know P in order to calculate λ_A. Also, it should always be kept in mind that the purpose in obtaining exact numerical solutions to this and the previous problems was to gain a firm grasp of the theory. Experimental work has not yet advanced to the stage where the precision of the formulas based on the linear model can be adequately evaluated, although enough studies have been finished to indicate that they are at least approximately correct in the cases where colonization occurs rapidly.

PROBLEM. How long would it take for the denuded island to regain 90 percent of its original species *composition*? (Think a bit about the wording of this question and attempt some response before going on.)

ANSWER. The theory simply does not cover this question. Only the *number* of species is covered, not the actual identity, i.e., the composition, of the species. Do you see the difference? It would be possible to answer the composition question by an elaboration of the linear model, but complex probability theory would be involved, and no one has tried to do it yet. Surely a very long time would pass, on the average, before the new flora would hold 90 percent of its species in common with the old, and this would be only a temporary condition. Do you understand why?

AREA AND DISTANCE EFFECTS

It is easy to see that a larger island should have more species at equilibrium than a smaller island which is at the same distance from the same source area (Figure 6). This AREA EFFECT (which we have already seen exemplified in the area-species curves) is due to the fact that the small island holds smaller populations, which are subject to more frequent extinction. The λ_S curve is about the same for both islands, because they are equally distant to the source area and receive about the same number of colonists from it; also the number of species in the source area, P, is the same for both islands.

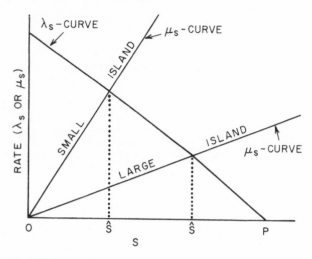

6   AREA EFFECT. An increase in land area lowers the extinction curve and, therefore, raises the number of species at equilibrium.

Next, we can deduce the result of the reverse situation, where the area of the two islands is the same, but one island is closer to the source island than the other. In this case the closer island should have a larger number of species at equilibrium (Figure 7). The a priori basis for predicting this DISTANCE EFFECT is the expected smaller rate of immigration onto the more distant island.

If you now understand all the reasoning behind the turnover equation and the prediction of the area and distance effects, you are prepared to employ equilibrium theory in a more flexible way. For example, try the following two problems.

PROBLEM. In a real experiment, a series of very small mangrove islands in the Florida Keys were denuded of their insect faunas by fumigation with methyl bromide, and the recolonization was then closely observed. The fauna of the most distant island regained its old equilibrium number more slowly than was the case for several other faunas located nearer the source areas. By studying the equations based on the linear equilibrium model, how could you have predicted this effect? (*Hint:* you won't be able to deduce it from the graphical models alone.)

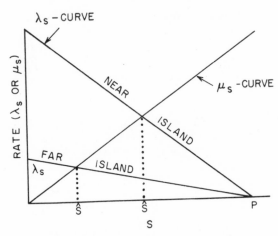

7   DISTANCE EFFECT. An increase in distance from the source of immigrant species lowers the immigration curve and, therefore, decreases the number of species at equilibrium.

ANSWER. Look at Equation 3. Distant islands should have a smaller λ_A, simply because fewer propagules are able to reach them. According to the strict terms of the linear model, μ_A should not vary with distance. This means that the term $e^{-(\lambda_A + \mu_A)t}$ approaches zero more slowly as t increases, and consequently S approaches $\hat{S}$ $[= \lambda_A P/(\lambda_A + \mu_A)]$ more slowly on the more distant island.

PROBLEM. Suppose a large island and a small island are equidistant from the source area. Would they reach equilibrium at the same time? If not, which would reach equilibrium first?

ANSWER. Look at Equation 3 again and think about the relation of μ_A to area. The smaller island should have a larger μ_A and hence should approach equilibrium faster.

PROBLEM. Two islands, one large and one small, are otherwise similar; in particular they have similar environments and are located the same distance from the same source region. A bird species colonizes both islands in the same year. On which island are the colonists more likely to evolve to endemic status?

ANSWER. The equilibrium theory predicts that the colonists are more likely to reach endemic status on the larger island. The reason for this result may not have been immediately obvious to you. An examination of the graphical analysis that led to the "area effect" will show that the larger island, with its higher $\hat{S}$, has a lower μ_A, that is, a lower average extinction rate ($=$ slope of the μ_S curve). A lower average extinction rate means a longer average survival time per species, and hence a greater chance that any given population will persist long enough to evolve into an endemic species. In fact, it turns out to be generally true that within a single archipelago the percentage of endemic species on a given island, and not just the absolute number of endemic species, increases with the area of the island.

PROBLEM. This exercise is directed at students with a particular interest in graphical analysis. Even if you cannot solve it, study the answer supplied afterward to understand this kind of approach. The problem is to predict the shape of the colonization curve through time, from the beginning of immigration to the attainment of equilibrium.

ANSWER. The graphs in Figure 8 are nearly self-explanatory. The rate at which the number of species (S) present is increasing (dS/dt) is simply the difference between the rates at which new species are arriving (I) and old ones are going extinct (E). When $E = I$, dS/dt is equal to zero, and equilibrium exists by definition. The number of species present follows a rising curve, as shown in the right-hand figure. The rate at which this curve ascends, however, is continually decreasing, because I and E converge toward each other from the beginning, and their difference $(dS/dt$

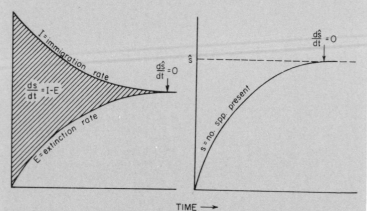

TIME →

8   SHAPE OF COLONIZATION CURVE. As an empty island is colonized, the immigration rate decreases and the extinction rate increases until the two are equal, producing species equilibrium (*left*). The colonization curve is obtained as the summed difference, through time, between immigration and extinction (*right*).

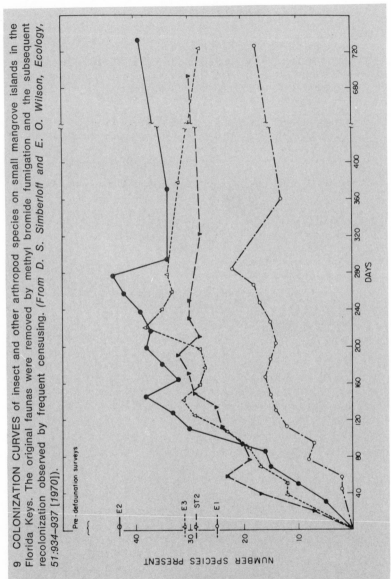

9 COLONIZATION CURVES of insect and other arthropod species on small mangrove islands in the Florida Keys. The original faunas were removed by methyl bromide fumigation and the subsequent recolonization observed by frequent censusing. *(From D. S. Simberloff and E. O. Wilson, Ecology, 51:934–937 [1970]).*

$= I - E)$ is therefore always decreasing. To be more precise, the number of species present on the island is the integral through time of $I - E$, a value whose rate of increase is always decreasing with time. Some actual examples of colonization curves are shown in Figure 9.

Suggested Additional Reading

Darlington, P. J. 1957. ZOOGEOGRAPHY: THE GEOGRAPHICAL DISTRIBU-
TION OF ANIMALS. John Wiley & Sons, Inc., New York. $xi + 675$
pp. (The classic empirical study of vertebrate zoogeography,
containing discussions of faunal balance and turnover on the
global scale.)

MacArthur, R. H. and E. O. Wilson. 1967. THE THEORY OF ISLAND
BIOGEOGRAPHY. Princeton University Press, Princeton, N.J. $xi +$
203 pp. (A theoretical study that derives many of the results of
biogeography, and in particular the species equilibrium, from
first principles in population and community ecology.)

Pielou, E. C. 1969. AN INTRODUCTION TO MATHEMATICAL ECOLOGY.
Interscience Publishers, New York. $viii + 286$ pp. (Although
primarily devoted to ecology, Pielou's textbook covers several
topics in dispersal and patterns of distribution of organisms not
adequately treated in the other two books cited above.)

Glossary

$a_1, a_2, a_3, \ldots, a_n$ symbols designating alleles that occur on the same locus in the population.

A in population genetics, a symbol designating a particular allele; in species equilibrium theory, the area of an island.

α competition coefficient; the amount by which each individual diminishes the growth of the competing species.

b the individual birth rate, the number of female offspring one female will have per unit of time.

β competition coefficient; same as α.

d the individual death rate, the average number of deaths per individual per unit of time (if one in ten die in a day, for example, $d = 0.1$ individuals per individual per day).

Δq the amount of change, from 0 to 1, that occurs in q, the frequency of an allele, in one generation.

e the base of natural logarithms, a constant with a value of 2.71828. . . .

H the entropy measure of diversity; the negative sum of the frequencies of each category multiplied by the logarithms of the frequencies.

H_s the entropy measure of species diversity; based on the number of organisms found in each species for all species in the sample.

h^2 heritability; the fraction of the variance in a given characteristic of a population that is due to genetic variation in the population.

l_x survivorship; the proportion of females surviving to age x.

λ_A the average immigration rate of species; in other words, λ_S (see below) divided by S, the number of species present.

λ_S the immigration rate of species; the rate at which new species are arriving on an island per unit time when S species are already present.

ln "the natural logarithm of," where the base of the logarithm is e.

log "the logarithm of," where the base can be e, 10, or any other value chosen for convenience.

m the migration rate in population genetics; the fraction (from 0 to 1) of a population that consists of individuals that immigrated to it from other populations.

m_x the fecundity at age x; specifically, the average number of daughters each female will produce at age x.

μ the "forward" mutation rate; the fraction of a given allele that mutates in each generation to a second given allele; the value can range from 0 to 1.

μ_A the average extinction rate of species; in other words, μ_S (see below) divided by S, the number of species present.

μ_S the extinction rate of species; the number of species becoming extinct per unit time on an island when S species are present.

n the number of generations or the number of chromosomes.

N the number of organisms in the population; often referred to as the "size" or "abundance" of the population.

ν the reverse mutation rate; the fraction of a given allele that mutates each generation to a second given allele, but in the opposite direction from that given by the forward mutation rate μ (in other words from a to A instead of A to a).

p the frequency of a given allele on one locus throughout the whole population, a value that can range from 0 to 1 (if 20 percent of all the alleles on a locus are A, then p of A is 0.20; another way of making this statement is $p_{(A)} = 0.20$). See also q.

p_0 the frequency of a given allele at the starting generation (generation number zero).

$\hat{p}$ the frequency of a given allele at equilibrium, in other words when no further evolution is occurring.

$p(x)$ the probability that some quantity will be exactly equal to x.

P the number of species in the "pool," i.e., the number of species found in surrounding areas that are capable of immigrating to a given island.

q the frequency of a given allele on one locus throughout the whole population, a value that can range from 0 to 1 (if 80 percent of all the alleles on a locus are a, then q of a is 0.80; another way of making this statement is $q_{(a)} = 0.80$). See also p, and note that $p + q = 1$.

q_0 the frequency of a given allele at the starting generation (generation number zero).

q_n the frequency of a given allele at the nth generation, in other words n generations after the starting generation.

$\hat{q}$ the frequency of a given allele at equilibrium, in other words when no further evolution is occurring.

r the intrinsic rate of increase; the fraction by which a population increases in size in each unit of time.

R_0 the net reproductive rate or replacement rate; the average number of females produced in the next generation by each female in the present generation.

s the selection coefficient; the relative rate by which the frequency of a given genotype is reduced each generation by selection.

S the number of species.

$\hat{S}$ the number of species at equilibrium.

t amount of time elapsed. This can be expressed in minutes, hours, days, years, generations, or whatever unit is convenient.

v_x the reproductive value; the relative number of female offspring that will be produced by each female that survives to age x.

W the fitness of a given genotype; the relative rate by which the frequency of a given genotype is increased each generation by selection.

$\overline{W}$ the average fitness of a set of genotypes belonging to the same population.

Index